COGNITIVE PROCESSES in WRITING

BF 456
W8
C63

COGNITIVE
PROCESSES
in WRITING

Edited by

LEE W. GREGG
ERWIN R. STEINBERG
Carnegie-Mellon University

LEA LAWRENCE ERLBAUM ASSOCIATES, PUBLISHERS
1980 Hillsdale, New Jersey

SEP 7 1983

344554

Copyright © 1980 by Lawrence Erlbaum Associates, Inc.
All rights reserved. No part of this book may be reproduced in
any form, by photostat, microform, retrieval system, or any other
means, without the prior written permission of the publisher.

Lawrence Erlbaum Associates, Inc., Publishers
365 Broadway
Hillsdale, New Jersey 07642

Library of Congress Cataloging in Publication Data

Main entry under title:

Cognitive processes in writing.

   Bibliography: p.
   Includes index.
   1. Writing—Psychological aspects   2. English
language—Rhetoric.   3. Cognition.   I. Gregg, Lee W.,
II. Steinberg, Erwin R.
BF456.W8C63   808.042′019   80-18624
ISBN 0-89859-032-9

Printed in the United States of America

Contents

Preface

This book originally began as a set of questions posed by faculty on the campus of Carnegie-Mellon University:

What do we know about how people write?
What do we need to know to help people write better?

In the ensuing discussions among interested members of the Department of Psychology and the Department of English, we arrived at some general propositions:

1. Discovering how people write is an interdisciplinary problem that probably should involve people from psychology, English, and linguistics.
2. The necessary research will probably best be undertaken by interdisciplinary teams.
3. Before we undertake too much research, we ought to find out:
   a. what research has already shown, and
   b. what research is now going on so that we can plan rationally for the necessary future research.

In May, 1978, therefore, we ran at Carnegie-Mellon an interdisciplinary symposium on "Cognitive Processes in Writing"; the papers from that symposium are in this volume. When it became clear at the symposium that others who attended were making useful contributions, we invited several of them to prepare chapters for inclusion here.

This book, therefore, presents a reasonably good picture of much of what research has shown about how people write, of what people are currently trying to find out, and of what needs to be done. Not all of the important research, either completed or current, has been included; we do not mean to suggest either that what has been left out is not important or that what we have included is necessarily more important than studies that we have not reported. As we have indicated, this volume reflects our interests and the interests of those who attended our symposium.

We think, however, that the chapters in this book give a fair picture of the kinds of things "we know," and we hope that as a result it will prove a useful stimulus for further research on cognitive processes in writing.

In concluding, we want to record here our debt to J. R. Hayes, Linda Flower, Sandra Bond, and Joyce Hannah, without whose help neither the symposium nor this book would have occurred.

LEE W. GREGG
ERWIN R. STEINBERG

ACKNOWLEDGMENTS

Individual papers in the volume were prepared under the sponsorship of various grants and contracts. The work by Flower and Hayes, Chapters 1 and 2, was supported in part by the National Institute of Education under Grant NIE-G-78-0195 and, in part, under Contract NIE-400-78-0043. The research on a process theory of writing by Allan Collins was supported under Contract NIE-400-76-0116. The paper by Carl Bereiter was prepared in connection with an NIE conference on problems in writing. The symposium was supported by a grant from the Buhl Foundation for the design and implementation of a core curriculum in Humanities and Social Sciences.

COGNITIVE PROCESSES in WRITING

I THEORETICAL APPROACHES

1 Identifying the Organization of Writing Processes

John R. Hayes
Linda S. Flower
Carnegie-Mellon University

Many have recognized that attention to process is potentially very important for the teaching of writing (Britton, Burgess, Martin, McLeod, & Rosen, 1975; Young, Becker, & Pike, 1970). Unfortunately, relatively few researchers have actually studied writing processes experimentally. Although noteworthy exceptions may be found in the work of Emig (1971), Zollner (1969), and Harding (1963), it is still true, as Britton et al. (1975) say, that "there has been very little systematic direct observation of fluent writers at work [p. 19]."

Cognitive psychologists have developed the technique of protocol analysis as a powerful tool for the identification of psychological processes (Newell & Simon, 1972). Although protocol analysis has most typically been used to identify processes in problem-solving tasks, as we will see, it can be used to identify processes in writing as well.

In this chapter:

1. We describe the technique of protocol analysis.[1]
2. We show how it can be used to identify writing processes.
3. We describe some early results in identifying writing processes that we obtained through its use.

---

[1]For those who are unfamiliar with protocol analysis, we describe it. For those who are familiar with protocol analysis but distrust it as a scientific method, we try to allay some of their worries. Instructions to the reader to attempt or complete certain exercises are intended to help the reader understand the principles involved.

WHAT IS A PROTOCOL?

A protocol is a description of the activities, ordered in time, which a subject engages in while performing a task.

A protocol, then, is a description, but not every description of a task performance is a protocol. Often we describe tasks mentioning only their outcomes or goals. We may say, for example, "My Great Dane, Spot, convinced me to give him his supper." This description tells us that the dog did one or more things to get food, but it doesn't say what these things were or in what order they occurred. That description, therefore, is *not* a protocol. The following description *is* a protocol, however.

Experimenter:	[seated at dinner table cutting into his steak]
Spot:	[seated directly behind the experimenter, his chin resting on the experimenter's shoulder. Spot watches intently as the steak is being cut.]
Experimenter:	[skewers a large piece of steak with his fork]
Spot:	[tail wags, stomach rumbles ominously]
Experimenter:	[begins to raise fork to mouth]
Spot:	[places paw on experimenter's arm and looks intently into experimenter's eyes]
Experimenter:	"Spot!"
Spot:	[removes paw, continues to watch intently]
Spot:	[drools into experimenter's shirt pocket]
Experimenter:	[abandons own dinner and feeds dog]

This is a protocol because it lists the activities that Spot engaged in and the order in which they occurred. In the same way, when we collect protocols of people solving problems, we are interested not just in the answers they give us, but, also and more important, in the sequence of things they do to get those answers. For example, they may draw diagrams, make computations, ask questions, and so forth, and they do those things in a particular order.

VERBAL PROTOCOLS

In a verbal, or "thinking aloud" protocol, subjects are asked to say aloud everything they think and everything that occurs to them while performing the task, no matter how trivial it may seem. Even with such explicit instructions, however, subjects may forget and fall silent—completely absorbed in the task. At such times the experimenter will say, "Remember, tell me everything you are thinking." Figure 1.1 shows a typical thinking-aloud protocol for a subject solving a water jug problem.

Water jug problems require the subject to measure out a specified quantity of water using three jugs, as shown in Fig. 1.2. None of the jugs has calibration

Water Jug Problem:

Given Jug A, which contains 9 quarts; Jug B, 42 quarts; and Jug C, 6 quarts; measure out exactly 21 quarts.

Protocol:

1. Uh, the first thing that's apparent is half of B is, is the uh, the
2. amount that you want.
3. *Exp:* Uh huh.
4. Um, you can't get 21 from just multiplying up A or C.
5. You get 18 and 18 respectively, that's as close as you can get,
6. I guess. Um, so I'll try to think of the different combinations that
7. might . . . come up with a surplus . . . or deficit of the 21 quarts . . . and
8. 9 and 6 are, 15 . . . if you took two 9's and two 6's, you'd have 30 which
9. would leave you . . . and pour them into the 42 container, you'd have a,
10. an open space of a, 12, which means nothing. How about . . . see . . . now I'm
11. trying to think of how close to 42 you can get with a 9 and the 6 quantities.
12. You can get . . . I forget the 7 table. It's been a long time since I've
13. had to multiply or anything so you'll have to give me some time. Um,
14. 9 times 5 is 45 . . . hm, 6 times 7 is 42, I think. Is that right?
15. *Exp:* Uh huh.
16. OK, so you can, uh . . . fill B with C, evenly . . .
17. *Exp:* You could . . .
18. So . . . if you were to take . . . 36 . . . hm, oh, uh, 6 times 4 is 24, and if you, uh,
19. What I'm trying to get rid of is, is, 3 quarts there . . .
20. *Exp:* Good.
21. So if you were to, um . . . still 24. I, I was trying to think possibly,
22. some way of . . . the difference between the 6 and 9 is 3 quarts. I
23. was trying to think of . . . a way to uh . . . oh, how about . . . you put the 3, 6
24. quart quantity into the 42 bottle, which is 18, then the runoff, from
25. pouring a 9 into a 6 which is 3 and 18 is 21.
26. *Exp:* Good.

FIG. 1.1.   Protocol of a water jug problem.

marks. That is, there are no marks indicating a one quart level, a two quart level, etc. The subject is told only how much each jug will hold when it is full.

One typical water jug problem requires the subject to measure out 31 quarts when: jug A will hold 20 quarts; jug B, 59 quarts; and jug C, 4 quarts. The problem can be solved in four steps as follows:

1. Fill Jug B.
2. Fill Jug A from Jug B, leaving 39 quarts in B.
3. Fill Jug C from B, leaving 35 quarts in B.
4. Empty C and fill it again from B, leaving the desired quantity, 31 quarts, in B.

Jug A   Jug B   Jug C

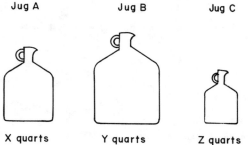

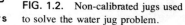

X quarts   Y quarts   Z quarts

FIG. 1.2. Non-calibrated jugs used to solve the water jug problem.

It is helpful when you analyze a protocol to have done the task yourself beforehand. So, before beginning to analyze the protocol in Fig. 1.1, try to solve the following problem.

> Measure 100 quarts given Jug A, holding 21 quarts; Jug B, holding 127 quarts; and Jug C, 3 quarts.

When you finish this problem, solve the problem in Fig. 1.1 if you have not already done so.

AN EXAMPLE OF PROTOCOL ANALYSIS

Now, let's examine the protocol in Fig. 1.1 in detail and try to make some reasonable guesses about what the subject was doing.

In his first sentence, the subject mentions something that appears to be irrelevant to solving the problem. He mentions the fact that the desired amount (21 quarts) is just half the quantity contained in Jug B. Now, division is a very useful operation in many algebra problems. In this problem, if we could divide Jug B in half, the problem would be solved. But alas! There is no division operation in water jug problems. All we can do is add and subtract the quantities in Jugs A, B, and C. Why, then, does the subject notice that the desired quantity is half of B? The simplest answer seems to be that he is confusing water jug problems (perhaps because he isn't thoroughly familiar with them) with the more general class of algebra problems. If this answer is correct, we would expect that the subject would stop noticing division relations as he gains more experience with water jug problems. In fact, that is what happened.

On line 3, the experimenter (Exp.) does just what the experimenter is supposed to do—that is, he is noncommittal. In general, the experimenter should answer only essential questions and remind the subject to keep talking.

From lines 4 and 5, we can guess that the subject has successively added 9's to get 9, 18, 27 . . . and 6's to get 6, 12, 18, 24 . . . and realized that neither sequence includes 21. From lines 6 through 10, we can see that the subject begins to consider combinations of 9's and 6's that may be added together to obtain interesting sums or that may be subtracted from the 42 quart container to obtain interesting differences. While considering sums, the subject fails to notice that the sum 6 + 6 + 9 solves the problem.

In lines 11 through 14, the subject tries to find out if 42 quarts can be obtained by adding 9's and 6's. The answer is "yes," but it doesn't help the subject to find a solution. It appears to be a "blind alley." In this section, the subject indicates several times that he doesn't feel confident about multiplication.

In lines 15 and 17, the experimenter provides the subject with a small amount of information by confirming his uneasy suspicion that 6 times 7 equals 42. On occasion, the experimenter must decide whether or not to provide information the subject requests. In this case, because the experimenter was really interested in water jug problems rather than in arithmetic, he decided to supply an arithmetic fact.

In lines 18 and 19, the subject realizes that if he had a way to subtract 3 quarts from 24 quarts, he could solve the problem. In line 20, the experimenter appears to slip by providing the subject with approval when he would better have remained silent. In line 21, the subject is still thinking of working from 24 quarts. In line 22, he discovers a way to add (rather than subtract) 3 quarts by pouring A into C and catching the overflow. In lines 23 and 24, he decides to work from 18 quarts rather than 24 quarts and then (on line 25) immediately solves the problem.

Now, let's stand back from the details of the protocol to see if we can characterize the whole problem-solving process that the subject engaged in. Before reading further, review the discussion of the protocol and then try to characterize the problem-solving process yourself.

One way to characterize the problem-solving process is to describe it as a search for an operator or a combination of operators to solve the problem. (In this case, the operators are arithmetic procedures such as division and subtraction). In Fig. 1.3, where we have diagrammed this search process, we can see that search proceeds, generally, from simple to complex—that is, from single operators to complex combinations of operators.

Until line 18, the subject's search for a solution could have been guided by the problem statement previously described. That is, by reading the problem statement, the subject could have decided that what was needed to solve the problem was some combination of algebraic operators. Until line 18, he could simply be trying one combination after another. We call this sort of search "forward search"; that is, it is search suggested by the problem statement alone. In lines 18 and 19, however, the subject formulates a goal on the basis of his difficulties in solving the problem. He notes that he hasn't been able to get closer than 3 quarts to the answer and attempts to find an operator that will subtract 3 quarts. This goal depends not just on the problem statement but also on the subject's experience in trying to solve the problem—that is, on his distance from the goal. It is a

Lines of Protocol	Operator Applied	Outcome	Comment
1–2	Divide by 2.	Fail	Operator not available.
4–5	Add 9's.	Fail	
4–5	Add 6's.	Fail	The subject apparently doesn't try all com-
6–8	Add 9's and 6's.	Fail	binations because he fails to notice that $6 + 6 + 9 = 21$.
7–10	Add 9's and 6's and Subtract from 42.	Fail	
18–19	Notice difficulty.	Succeed	The subject notices the operators above got him no closer to 21 than 24; he sets the goal of finding an operator to subtract 3.
22	Overflow 9 into 6.	Fail	
23–25	Add 6 three times and overflow 9 into 6.	Succeed	

Forward Search *(bracket spanning lines 1–2 through 7–10)*

Means–Ends Analysis *(bracket spanning lines 18–19 through 23–25)*

FIG. 1.3.   Analysis of water jug protocol.

form of means–ends analysis in which the subject attempts to find a means to the end of reducing his distance from the goal.

The whole solution process then consists of:

1. An initial phase of forward search through an increasingly complex sequence of operators, followed by
2. A phase of means–ends analysis in which the subject succeeds in finding a solution.

In analyzing a protocol, we attempt to describe the psychological processes that a subject uses to perform a task. To do this, it is useful to be familiar both with the properties of the task and with the problem solver's component psychological processes. In analyzing the foregoing water jug protocol, knowing that the task required algebraic operators and that human problem solvers often use processes of forward search and means–ends analysis helped us to recognize how the subject had organized these processes in his search for a solution. In the same way, when we analyze other protocols, knowledge of other tasks and of other psychological properties will be useful. This is not to say that we must already understand a performance before we can analyze it. It is just that when we do understand some things about the performance, we can use them very profitably to learn other things.

When we analyze the following water jug protocol, knowledge of the psychological phenomenon of set is very helpful. The problem used in this protocol can be solved in either of two ways. It can be solved by the procedure $B-A-2C$, or it can be solved by the simpler procedure $A-C$. Just before solving this problem, the subject worked a series of six problems, all of which required the procedure $B-A-2C$ for solution. As a result, we would expect the subject to show a set to use the $B-A-2C$ procedure. As lines 6 through 9 show, however, the subject actually solves the problem by the $A-C$ procedure. Nevertheless, if we look back to 3 and 4, we see that the subject's first problem-solving attempt was to subtract A from B, which suggests that he started to use the $B-A-2C$ procedure even though he didn't carry it through. Clearly, analyzing the protocol gives us evidence about the subject's solution process that we can't get just by looking at the subject's answer.

PROTOCOL ANALYSIS — MORE GENERALLY CONSIDERED

As we have seen, protocol analysis can be used as an aid in understanding a wide variety of tasks from simple problem solving in apes to complex performances such as chess playing in humans. Typically though, protocols are incomplete. Many processes occur during the performance of a task that the subject can't or doesn't report. The psychologist's task in analyzing a protocol is to take the incomplete record that the protocol provides together with his knowledge of the nature of the task and of human capabilities and to infer from these a model of the underlying psychological processes by which the subject performs the task.

Analyzing a protocol is like following the tracks of a porpoise, which occasionally reveals itself by breaking the surface of the sea. Its brief surfacings are like the glimpses that the protocol affords us of the underlying mental process.

1. Uh, . . .I'm adding and subtracting here.
2. *Exp:* Say what you're adding and subtracting.
3. O.K. Well, 23 from 49 . . . is . . . uh . . . reminds me when
4. we keep score when we play cards. 26 . . . oh, OK. Er it
5. would be easy enough. You take . . . um . . . OK. How do we
6. get this into water and jugs now? . . . because you could take a . . .
7. which is 23, and pour it into C which is 3, there we go,
8. pour it into C which is 3, and 20 would be what would go . . .
9. right into B.
10. *Exp:* Good.

FIG. 1.4. A water jug protocol.

Between surfacings, the mental process, like the porpoise, runs deep and silent. Our task is to infer the course of the process from these brief traces.

The power of protocol analysis lies in the richness of its data. Even though protocols are typically incomplete, they provide us with much more information about processes by which tasks are performed than does simply examining the outcome of the process. Knowing what answer people get in solving problems is much less informative than catching even fragmentary glimpses of the complex processes by which they arrive at the answer.

ANALYSIS OF A WRITING PROTOCOL

In this section, we first describe a model of expository writing. Then we apply the model in analyzing a protocol by a writer who is especially clear in commenting about and identifying his writing processes. The degree to which the processes identified through protocol analysis correspond to the processes identified by the writer provide a test of the model.

A Model of the Writing Process Derived Through Protocol Analysis

Although space does not permit us to describe our research in detail, we have analyzed a number of writing protocols over the last 2 years. The results of this research have led us to propose the tentative model of the writing process diagrammed in Fig. 1.5.

The Model

The unique features of the model are:

1. It identifies not only subprocesses of the composing process, but also the organization of those subprocesses.
2. Minor variations in its simple control structure (shown in Fig. 1.10) allow it to describe individual differences in composing styles.

Although the model is provisional, it provides a first approximate description of normal composition that can guide research and afford a valuable starting point in the search for more refined models.

To facilitate our analysis of writing, we have divided the writer's world into three major parts: the task environment, the writer's long-term memory, and the writing process. Our model describes the writing process. The task environment and the writer's long-term memory are the context in which the model operates.

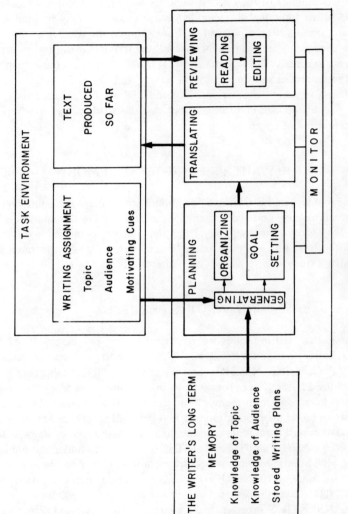

FIG. 1.5. Structure of the writing model.

THE TASK ENVIRONMENT

The task environment includes everything outside the writer's skin that influences the performance of the task. It includes the writing assignment, that is, a description of the topic and the intended audience, and it may include information relevant to the writer's motivation. For example, the teacher's stern expression when he presents an assignment may tell the writer that the assignment must be taken very seriously. Britton et al. (1975) have emphasized the importance of such motivational factors. Once writing has begun, the task environment also includes the text which the writer has produced so far. This text is a very important part of the task environment because the writer refers to it repeatedly during the process of composition.

THE WRITER'S LONG-TERM MEMORY

We assume that writers have knowledge about many topics, e.g., auto mechanics and American history, and about many audiences, e.g., children and Catholics, stored in long-term memory. They may also have generalized writing plans, perhaps in the form of a story grammar (Rumelhart, 1975) or a formula such as the journalist's questions, "who, what, where, when, why?"

THE WRITING PROCESS

We propose that writing consists of three major processes: PLANNING, TRANSLATING, and REVIEWING. The PLANNING process consists of GENERATING, ORGANIZING, and GOAL-SETTING subprocesses. The function of the PLANNING process is to take information from the task environment and from long-term memory and to use it to set goals and to establish a writing plan to guide the production of a text that will meet those goals. The plan may be drawn in part from long-term memory or may be formed anew within the PLANNING process. The TRANSLATING process acts under the guidance of the writing plan to produce language corresponding to information in the writer's memory. The function of the REVIEWING process, which consists of READING and EDITING subprocesses, is to improve the quality of the text produced by the TRANSLATING process. It does this by detecting and correcting weaknesses in the text with respect to language conventions and accuracy of meaning, and by evaluating the extent to which the text accomplishes the writer's goals. The structures of the various processes are shown in Figs. 1.6 through 1.10.

Planning: Generating.   The function of the GENERATING process is to retrieve information relevant to the writing task from long-term memory. We assume that this process derives its first memory probe from information about the topic and the audience presented in the task environment. Because each retrieved item is used as the new memory probe, items are retrieved from memory in associative chains. In order to focus search on relevant material, the retrieval chain is broken whenever an item is retrieved that is not useful to the writing task. Search is then restarted with a new memory probe derived from the task environment or from useful material already retrieved.

Some criterion for terminating search chains is essential to prevent the process from getting lost in associative reverie. The criterion that we have chosen, i.e., one irrelevant item, may have to be relaxed somewhat to simulate human performance accurately. We believe, though, that it won't have to be relaxed much beyond one item. The most persistent memory searches we have observed in writing protocols never extended more than three retrievals beyond useful material.

When an item is retrieved, the GENERATING process may produce a note. Characteristically, these notes are single words or sentence fragments, although

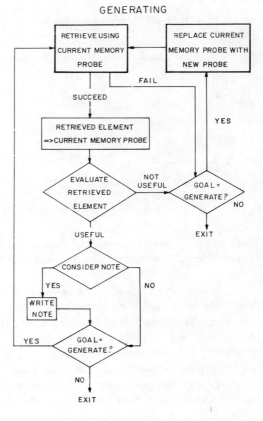

FIG. 1.6. The structure of the GENERATING process.

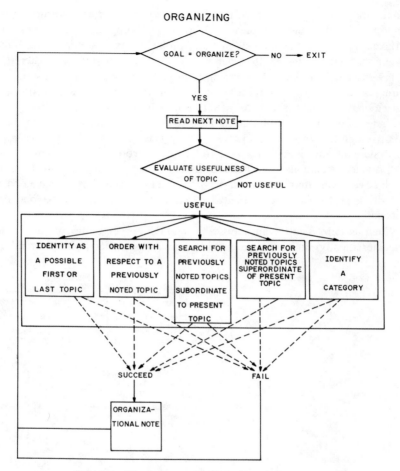

FIG. 1.7.   The structure of the ORGANIZING process.

they may sometimes be complete sentences. The form of these notes will be used later to identify occurrences of the GENERATING process.

Planning: Organizing.   The function of the ORGANIZING process is to select the most useful of the materials retrieved by the GENERATING process and to organize them into a writing plan. The plan may be structured either temporally (e.g., "First, I'll say A, then B.") or hierarchically (e.g., "Under topic #1, I should discuss A, B, and C.") or both.

Organizing is done by the elementary operators shown in Fig. 1.7. The first four of these operators act on single topics or pairs of topics; e.g., the second operator decides which of two topics to discuss first. The last operator, "Identify a category," may act to classify a large number of topics that were generated separately under the same heading.

Notes generated by the ORGANIZING process often have an organizational form. That is, they are systematically indented, or numbered, or alphabetized, or possibly all of these. This organizational form will be used later to identify occurrences of the ORGANIZING process.

Planning: Goal Setting.   Some of the materials retrieved by the GENERAT-ING process are not topics to be written about but rather are criteria by which to judge the text. Often such criteria appear in the protocol when the writer is considering the audience or features of the text. At such times the writer may say, "Better keep it simple," or, "I need to write a transition here." The GOAL SETTING process identifies and stores such criteria for later use in EDITING.

Translating.   The function of the TRANSLATING process is to take material from memory under the guidance of the writing plan and to transform it into acceptable written English sentences. We assume that material in memory is stored as propositions but not necessarily as language. By a proposition, we understand a structure such as

$$[(\text{Concept A}) (\text{Relation B}) (\text{Concept C})]$$
$$\text{or}$$
$$[(\text{Concept D}) (\text{Attribute E})], \text{etc.},$$

where concepts, relations, and attributes are memory structures, perhaps complex networks or images, for which the writer may or may not have names.

To illustrate the operation of the TRANSLATING process (see Fig. 1.8), we have invented a scenario of a student writing an essay on Henri Rousseau.

1. Get next part of writing plan: "I've covered the early years, now I've got to say how he got into painting."
2. Plan next sentence: Retrieve propositions.
   Proposition A: [(Rousseau) (showed) (some early promise)]
   Proposition B: [(Rousseau) (did) (very little painting until 40)]
   Sentence plan: (Proposition A) but (Proposition B)
3. Express next proposition part: "Rousseau . . . Rousseau, what? Rousseau displayed . . . . Although Rousseau displayed some early promise . . . , etc."

Writing done during the TRANSLATING process shows two features:

1. Characteristically, it is in the form of complete sentences, and
2. It is often associated with a protocol segment that contains an interrogative

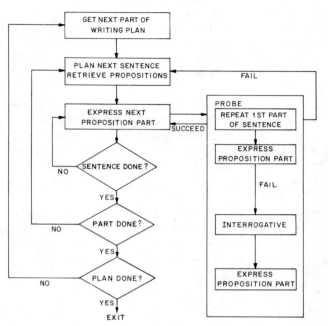

FIG. 1.8.   The structure of the TRANSLATING process.

reflecting search for the next sentence part, e.g., "Rousseau did what?" or, "How do I want to put this?"

These features will be used later to identify occurrences of the TRANSLATING process.

Reviewing.   The function of the reviewing process is to improve the quality of the written text. It consists, as Fig. 1.9 shows, of two subprocesses: READING and EDITING.

Reviewing: Editing.   The EDITING process examines any material that the writer puts into words, whether by reading, writing, or speaking. Its purpose is to detect and correct violations in writing conventions and inaccuracies of meaning and to evaluate materials with respect to the writing goals. These evaluations may be reflected in questions such as, "Will this argument be convincing?" and, "Have I covered all parts of the plan?"

REVIEWING

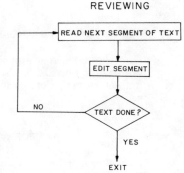

FIG. 1.9. The structure of the
REVIEWING process.

We assume that the EDITING process has the form of a production system.[2] The conditions of the productions have two parts. The first part specifies the kind of language to which the editing production applies, e.g., formal sentences, notes, etc. The second is a fault detector for such problems as grammatical errors, incorrect words, and missing context. When the conditions of a production are met, e.g., a grammatical error is found in a formal sentence, the action that is triggered is a procedure for fixing the fault.

Consider the following production:

[(formal sentence) (first letter of sentence lower case)
→ change first letter to upper case]

If the writer is producing formal sentences, this production will detect and correct errors in initial capitalization. However, if the writer is only producing notes, the conditions of the production will not be met and capitalization will be ignored.

Although the action in the preceding production is simple, in some cases the action may invoke the whole writing process recursively. For example, in one writing protocol, the writer's first draft contained the first sentence of the final draft immediately followed by the seventh sentence of the final draft. In editing

---

[2]A production system is an ordered sequence of condition–action rules. The left side of each rule shows the condition or stimulus, and the right side shows the action to be taken if the condition is met. The conditions are tested in order, starting with the first rule. The order of the productions is important. Consider the production system for putting a horse in a barn:

Conditions		Actions
(horse out of barn) and (barn door closed)	→	(open barn door)
(horse out of barn)	→	(put horse in barn)
(barn door open)	→	(close barn door)

Changing the order of these productions could have very serious consequences for the horse!

EDITING

EDIT FOR STANDARD LANGUAGE CONVENTIONS

[(formal or note)(spelling fault)   ⇒ fix spelling fault]
[(formal)(grammar fault)   ⇒ fix grammar fault]
[(formal)(repetition of word)   ⇒ search for alternative]
etc.

EDIT FOR ACCURACY OF MEANING

[(formal or note)(wrong word)   ⇒ fix word]
[(formal or note)(ambiguous word)   ⇒ remove ambiguity]
etc.

EVALUATE FOR READER UNDERSTANDING

[(formal)(unusual or technical word) ⇒ find more common word]
[(formal)(missing context)   ⇒ supply context]
etc.

EVALUATE FOR READER ACCEPTANCE

[(formal)(material offensive to reader) ⇒ soften]
[(formal)(tone inconsistent)   ⇒ make uniform]
etc.

FIG. 1.10.   The structure of the EDITING process showing alternative modes
of editing.

the first draft, the writer recognized that the reader would not have sufficient
context to understand the relation between these two sentences. To correct this
fault, the writer constructed a small explanatory essay to insert between the
sentences. Thus, in this case, the fixing procedure invoked the whole writing
process.

We assume that the EDITING process is triggered automatically whenever the
conditions of an editing production are satisfied and that it will interrupt any
other ongoing process.

We distinguish between REVIEWING and EDITING as two distinct modes of
behavior. On the one hand, EDITING is triggered automatically and may occur
in brief episodes interrupting other processes. REVIEWING, on the other hand,
is not a spur-of-the-moment activity but rather one in which the writer decides to
devote a period of time to systematic examination and improvement of the text. It

occurs typically when the writer has finished a translation process rather than as an interruption to that process.

The Monitor. The relations among the processes are defined by the simple production system shown in Fig. 1.11. The structure of the monitor was chosen to reflect three observations about composition processes.

1. The EDITING and GENERATING processes may interrupt other processes. Thus, the first two production rules triggering EDITING and GENERATING processes take priority over goal setting rules.

2. The writer's intuitions and the persistence of his or her actions suggest that writing processes are controlled by goals. Thus, if writers report that they are trying to organize material, they will persistently return to ORGANIZING processes even when those processes are interrupted by EDITING and GENERATING (productions 3 through 6 define the writer's goals).

3. Individual differences in goal setting reflect important individual differences in writing style. Figure 1.12 shows four alternative configurations for the goal setting productions. Each configuration corresponds to a characteristically different way of producing an essay. Configuration 1, for example, corresponds to a style in which the writer tries to produce a perfect first sentence and then to follow the perfect first sentence with a perfect second sentence and so on. The work of planning, translating, and reviewing each sentence is completed before the writer proceeds to the next sentence. With Configuration 2, thoughts are written down as they occur to the writer and he reviews them later. With Configuration 3, the writer tries to generate a perfect first draft. Configuration 4 yields a breadth-first composing process. A draft is planned and then written out in full before any review takes place. Lowenthal and Wason (1977) have described writing styles among academics that correspond to Configurations 3 and 4.

Rules 7 through 10 in Fig. 1.11 have the effect of executing the current goal when the goal activity is not being interrupted by rule 1 or rule 2.

As a final observation about the model, notice that the GENERATING process operates differently when the goal is GENERATING than when it is not. When the goal is GENERATING, the GENERATING process is persistent.

1. (Generated language in STM → edit)
2. (New information in STM → generate)
3.-6. Goal setting productions (These vary from writer to writer; see Fig. 1.12).
7. [(goal = generate) → generate]
8. [(goal = organize) → organize]
9. [(goal = translate) → translate]
10. [(goal = review) → review]

FIG. 1.11.   MONITOR

That is, each attempt to generate is followed by another attempt to generate. When the goal is not GENERATING, each attempt to generate is followed by a return to the process specified by the current goal (the one which GENERATING interrupted).

TESTING THE MODEL

We compare our model with a writing protocol in which the writer gave especially clear indications of ongoing writing processes and of the transitions between processes. (The writer's style suggests that he sets his goals in the same way as the monitor with Configuration 4—see Fig. 1.12.) This relatively unambiguous protocol provides a rigorous test of the model's adequacy.

The protocol consisted of 14 pages of verbal transcript (the thinking aloud part of the protocol), five pages of notes, and a page of completed essay. We divided the verbal transcript into a sequence of segments, each containing a simple comment or statement. We have analyzed the first 458 segments of the transcript, or about half of it.

The segments are of three general types:

Configuration 1 (Depth first)
3. [New element from translate   → (goal = review)]
4. [New element from organize   → (goal = translate)]
5. [New element from generate   → (goal = organize)]
6. [Not enough material   → (goal = generate)]

Configuration 2 (Get it down as you think of it, then review)
3. [New element from generate   → (goal = organize)]
4. [New element from organize   → (goal = translate)]
5. [Not enough material   → (goal = generate)]
6. [Enough material   → (goal = review)]

Configuration 3 (Perfect first draft)
3. [Not enough material   → (goal = generate)]
4. [Enough material, plan not complete → (goal = organize)]
5. [New element from translate   → (goal = review)]
6. [Plan complete   → (goal = translate)]

Configuration 4 (Breadth first)
3. [Not enough material   → (goal = generate)]
4. [Enough material, plan not complete → (goal = organize)]
5. [Plan complete   → (goal = translate)]
6. [Translation complete   → (goal = review)]

FIG. 1.12.   Alternate configuration for the monitor.

1. *Metacomments*—comments that writers make about the writing process itself, e.g., "I'll just make a list of topics now," "I'm gonna write out a draft," "Better go back and read it over."
2. *Task-oriented or "content" statements*—statements that reflect the application of writing processes to the current task, e.g., "That's not the right word" reflects an editing process; "I'll use that topic last" reflects an organizing process, etc.
3. *Interjections*—such as "OK," "Well, let's see," "all right," "umm," "ah," etc.

Consider the sequence of segments: Well,/I'll just make a list of topics now./ Energy conservation,/pollution,/unemployment. The first segment is an interjection; the second, a metacomment; and the rest are task-oriented statements. (Interjections were not analyzed in this study.)

Writing protocols are complex, and writers are often incomplete or ambiguous when they describe what they are doing. As a result, in analyzing a protocol, we frequently have to make judgments about the writer's meaning. The presence of such judgments may lead one to question the objectivity of the analyses. Because we are testing our model by comparing it to a protocol, we have to be especially careful to establish the objectivity of our analysis. To do this, we have taken the following steps:

1. Whenever objective evidence was available, we used it. Thus, reading and writing processes were identified by matching the verbal protocol word for word with the writer's notes and text (the objective evidence).
2. Whenever possible, processes were identified by using converging lines of evidence, e.g., the form of the written material on the one hand, and the writer's comments about what he is doing on the other.
3. The most important analyses were replicated by independent judges.

PROTOCOL SECTIONS

The writer's metacomments suggest that the protocol can be divided quite cleanly into three sections. In the first section, including segments 1 through 116, the writer's goal is to generate; in the second, including segments 117 through 270, it is to organize; and in the third, including segments 271 through 458, it is to translate. Here are the metacomments that led us to this conclusion:

Segment 2. "And what I'll do now is to simply jot down random thoughts. . ."
Segment 5. "Topics as they occur randomly are. . ."
Segment 48. "Organizing nothing as yet."

Segment 69. "Other things to think about in this random search are. . ."
Segment 117. "Now I think it's time to go back and read over the material and elaborate on its organization."
Segment 161. "Now this isn't the overall organization. This is just the organization of a subpart."
Segment 237. "There's an organization."
Segment 239. "Let's try and write something."
Segment 243. "Oh, no. We need more organizing."
Segment 269. "I can imagine the possibility of an alternate plan. . ."
Segment 271. "But let's build on this plan and see what happens with it."

If these assumptions about goals are correct, it follows from the model that the most frequent process in the first section will be GENERATING interrupted occasionally by EDITING; in the second, ORGANIZING interrupted by GENERATING and EDITING; and in the third, TRANSLATING interrupted by GENERATING and EDITING. Further, we can make three predictions about the protocol:

1. The form of the written material should vary from section to section corresponding to changes in process from section to section. Thus, in the first section, we expect the generating process to produce many single words, detached phrases, and incomplete sentences. In the second section, we expect the organizing process to produce material that is systematically indented, alphabetized, or numbered. In the third section, we expect the translating process to produce many complete sentences and some material associated in the verbal protocol with interrogatives suggesting search for sentence continuation.

2. The content statements in the protocol should reflect the distribution of processes just predicted, and

3. The generating process should be more persistent in section 1 than in sections 2 and 3.

HYPOTHESIS 1:
THE FORM OF THE WRITTEN MATERIALS

To test the first hypothesis, we wanted to determine if items written during the first section had a form consistent with the GENERATING process; items written during the second section, with the ORGANIZING process; and the items written during the third section, with the TRANSLATING process. For this purpose we identified all of the items written in the three protocol sections: 26 in the first section; 24 in the second; and 12 in the third. An item was a word, phrase, or sentence that was identifiable in the verbal protocol as being written during a single segment or several contiguous segments. It was, in effect, a short burst of writing.

Three raters were given the written material and verbal protocol and were asked independently to make the following judgments about each written item:

1. Does it have good form, i.e., is it a complete, grammatical sentence?
2. Is it part of a systematically indented, alphabetized, or numbered structure, i.e., does it appear to be part of an outline or structured plan of some sort?
3. Is it associated in the verbal protocol with an interrogative suggesting search for sentence completion?

Table 1.1 shows that there was excellent agreement among the raters in making these judgments. For each of the properties, Table 1.2 shows the proportion of items written during each section that were judged to have that property. An item was scored as having a property if two or more of the judges agreed that it did.

Items written during section 1 sometimes had good form but most usually had none of the three properties. Items written during section 2 typically showed the second property (indentation, etc.) but neither of the other properties. Two-thirds of the items written during section 3 were of good form and many were associated in the protocol with interrogatives. No items written in any other section were associated with an interrogative. These results are quite consistent with the view that GENERATING is the dominant process in section 1, ORGANIZING in section 2, and TRANSLATING in section 3, and thus provide strong support for Hypothesis 1.

HYPOTHESIS 2: CLASSIFYING "CONTENT" STATEMENTS

Our second hypothesis is that the content statements in the protocol will reflect differences in distribution of processes in the three protocol sections. As with our first hypothesis, we are looking for evidence that the writing processes we have

TABLE 1.1
Agreement Among Raters in Assigning Properties to Written Items

Agreement Between Raters	Question A	Question B	Question C
1 & 2	.935	.968	1.000
1 & 3	.935	.984	.952
2 & 3	.903	.968	.952
Average Inter-rater Agreement	.924	.973	.968

TABLE 1.2
Proportion of Written Items With Each Property

	Section 1	Section 2	Section 3
% good form	0.385	0.000	0.667
% indented, etc.	0.154	0.917	0.000
% interrogative	0.000	0.000	0.417

postulated turn up where they ought to, e.g., GENERATING should appear prominently when the writer says that his goal is to generate ideas, etc. In addition, we are looking for evidence that the EDITING and GENERATING processes interrupt the other processes as we have postulated. Again, the expected distribution of writing processes is, in the first section, GENERATING interrupted by EDITING; in the second, ORGANIZING interrupted by EDITING and GENERATING; and in the third, TRANSLATING interrupted by EDITING and GENERATING.

To test this hypothesis, each of the authors independently classified each segment in two ways:

In classification 1, each segment was judged as belonging to one of the following four categories: (a) interjections; (b) metacomments; (c) content statements; and (d) a combination of metacomments and content statements.

In classification 2, the authors made judgments as to which of the writing processes was most likely to have given rise to the segment. Four alternative writing processes were considered: GENERATING, ORGANIZING, TRANSLATING, and EDITING.

Because the protocol sections were identified by examining the writer's metacomments, we wanted to test Hypothesis 2 using only segments that were purely content statements with no component of metacomment. Therefore, in the following analysis, we have considered only those segments that both authors classified as pure content statements. Out of a total of 458 segments, 170 were identified as pure content statements; approximately 130 as interjections; 18

TABLE 1.3
Proportion of Segments Assigned to Each Process

	Section 1		Section 2		Section 3	
	Author 1	Author 2	Author 1	Author 2	Author 1	Author 2
% GENERATING	79.5	86.4	18.3	15.0	13.6	7.6
% ORGANIZING	0.0	2.3	66.7	73.3	0.0	0.0
% TRANSLATING	11.4	0.0	5.0	0.0	72.7	77.3
% EDITING	9.1	11.4	10.0	11.7	13.6	15.2

previously identified as "reads" were not judged; and the remainder were judged by one author or the other as being metacomments in part or whole.

The authors agreed in attributing writing processes in 144 or 84.7% of the 170 content statements. Table 1.3 shows that, despite some differences, the authors agree that the content statements in section 1 can be attributed mostly to GENERATING; in section 2, to ORGANIZING; and in section 3, to TRANSLATING. They also agree that approximately 10 to 15% of the segments in each section can be attributed to EDITING and that approximately 10 to 15% of segments in sections 2 and 3 can be attributed to GENERATING. The most important disagreement is that one author attributes some segments in sections 1 and 2 to TRANSLATING whereas the other does not.

Figure 1.13, which shows the processes author 2 attributed to the sequence of metacomments and content statements, illustrates two features of the protocol:

1. Interruptions of other processes by EDITING and GENERATING are frequent and widely distributed.
2. Even though in segment 117, the writer announced, "Now it's time to go back and read over the material and elaborate on its organization," apparently he doesn't do very much organizing until segment 153. The reason for this is that the writer is indeed reading (10 "reads" occurred in this interval), and the reading triggered some GENERATING and EDITING interrupts.

Because we made the judgments of process in the context of the whole protocol, one must be concerned that this context could have influenced our judgment. For example, we might have attributed a segment to GENERATING rather than to TRANSLATING if the segment occurred early in the protocol.

To determine if consistent judgments of process could be made without context, we conducted the following study. We selected 41 content statements from the protocol and typed them on cards. The cards were then shuffled and presented for judgment independently to two coders (not the authors). Coder 1 agreed with one of us in 67% of judgments and Coder 2, in 77% of judgments. Most of the disagreements (16 out of 22) involved judgments of EDITING. Many segments that the author attributed to EDITING the coders attributed to GENERATING. EDITING may be especially difficult to identify out of context because "edits" often present a comment on the previous segment or represent a change in a previous segment. It is difficult, for example, to see that segment 87, "I guess all elements are low level," indicates editing for redundancy unless one also sees segment 86, "even low level elements of writing." If we consider only segments that the author attributed to GENERATING, ORGANIZING, or TRANSLATING, we find that both coders agree with the author in 86% of cases. These high levels of agreement are very encouraging and suggest that even if judgments were made without context, our conclusions concerning Hypothesis 2 would be substantially the same. Overall, then, our results strongly support Hypothesis 2.

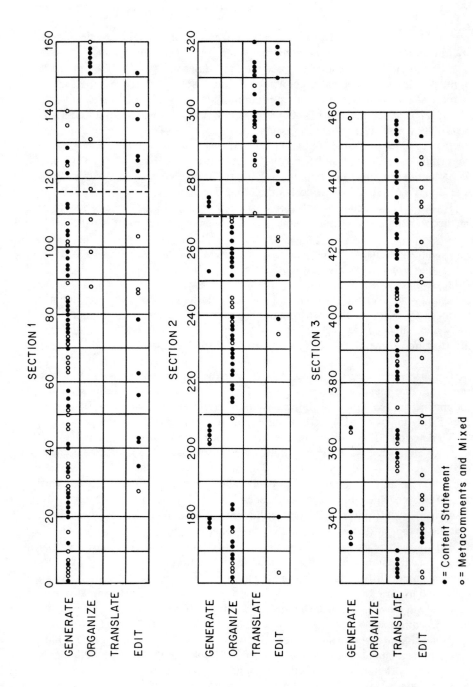

FIG. 1.13.   Processes attributed to segments by Author 2.

● = Content Statement

o = Metacomments and Mixed

26

HYPOTHESIS 3:
MEASURING RETRIEVAL CHAINS

Our third hypothesis is that the GENERATING process will be more persistent during section 1 of the protocol, when the goal is to generate, than during sections 2 and 3, when it is not. To test this hypothesis, one of the authors identified all of the content ideas generated during the protocol. (A single idea might be the topic of several protocol segments but was nonetheless counted as one idea.) A total of 48 separate ideas was identified. The two authors then independently judged whether each idea had been cued by the previous idea or not. Because the authors' judgments agreed in 96% of cases, we simply present the average of their results.

In section 1, 32 ideas occurred in chains of average length 6.4, whereas in sections 2 and 3, 16 ideas occurred in chains of average length 2.0. As the model predicted, the GENERATING process was much more persistent during the first section of the protocol than during the second two. The fact that the average chain length in sections 2 and 3 was two rather than one as the model requires suggests that our criteria for terminating search should be relaxed a bit.

The sequence in which ideas were retrieved in section 1 was strongly determined by associative connections, so we might expect the same sequence and the same associative connections to appear in the final essay. We might expect this *unless,* of course, an active ORGANIZING process intervenes between GENERATING and TRANSLATING as the model postulates.

Figure 1.14 shows the writer's outline for the essay as a structure of ideas in tree form. The numbers in the figure indicate the order in which the ideas were generated. Clearly, the retrieval order is very different from the outline order.

CONCLUSIONS

We have described protocol analysis and have demonstrated that it can be a powerful tool for the analysis of writing processes. We should emphasize, however, that we recommend it as a research tool for use in the laboratory. It is far too laborious a procedure to be used routinely in the classroom either for teaching or for evaluation.

We believe that the evidence provides very encouraging support for our model. All three of the model's predictions were strongly confirmed. We should note, however, that although these results are encouraging, they are quite limited in scope. First, although the model was derived through informal analysis of many protocols, it has been tested formally with only one protocol. Second, although the model is quite complex, only a few of its properties have been tested. We have tested some properties of the major writing processes, but we have not, for example, tested the model's predictions about individual dif-

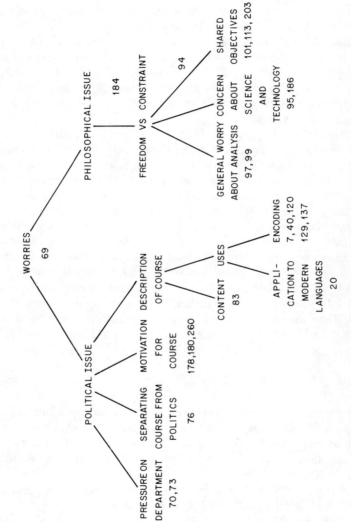

FIG. 1.14. The writer's plan and the protocol segments in which the ideas were generated.

28

ferences nor about the structure of the editing processes. We plan to conduct much more extensive testing of the model in the near future.

Whether or not it is supported by the data, one may still ask, "Is there really anything new about the model? Haven't English teachers been talking about processes such as planning, organizing, and editing for a long time?" Indeed, English teachers *have* been talking about such processes for a long time. Nonetheless, there is a great deal that is new about the model. First, the model is rather specific about the nature of the individual processes (see Figs. 1.6–1.10). Second, and more important, the model specifies the organization of these processes. In particular, it specifies an organization that is goal directed and recursive, that allows for process interrupts, and that can account for individual differences.

We should caution the reader not to interpret our model as a stage model. We are *not* saying that writing proceeds in order through successive stages of PLANNING, TRANSLATING, and REVIEWING. It *may* do so, and, indeed, in the part of the protocol examined in this paper, writing did proceed generally in successive stages. However, this is not the only sort of writing behavior we have observed, nor is it the only sort allowed by the model. The model is recursive and allows for a complex intermixing of stages. As we noted previously, the whole writing process, including PLANNING, TRANSLATING, and REVIEWING, may appear as a part of an EDITING subprocess. Because EDITING can interrupt any other process, these processes can appear within any other process.

Further, we should note that we do not intend to imply that all writers use all of the processes we have described. Our model is a model of competent writers. Some writers, though, perhaps to their disadvantage, may fail to use some of the processes. We have, for example, observed a writer who failed to organize. This writer, however, could not be viewed as competent.

We believe that our model, if it is approximately correct, can serve as a guide to the diagnosis of writing difficulties. We hope that, whether it is right or wrong, it can serve as "a target to shoot at," and hence a guide to further research on writing.

REFERENCES

Britton, J., Burgess, T., Martin, N., McLeod, A., & Rosen, H. *The development of writing abilities (11–18).* London: Macmillan, 1975.

Emig, J. *The composing processes of twelfth graders.* Champaign, Ill.: National Council of Teachers of English, 1971. (Research Report No. 13.)

Harding, D. W. *Experience into words.* London: Chath & Windus, 1963.

Lowenthal, D., & Wason, P. Academics and their writing. *Times Literary Supplement,* London, June 24, 1977.

Newell, A., & Simon, H. A. *Human problem solving.* Englewood Cliffs, N.J.: Prentice-Hall, 1972.

Rumelhart, D. Notes on a schema for stories. In D. Bobrow & A. Collins (Eds.), *Representation and understanding*. New York: Academic Press, 1975.

Young, R. E., Becker, A. L., & Pike, K. L. *Rhetoric: Discovery and change*. New York: Harcourt, Brace, & World, 1970.

Zollner, R. Talk-write: A behavioral pedagogy for composition. *College English*, 1969, *30*(1), 267–320.

2 The Dynamics of Composing: Making Plans and Juggling Constraints

Linda S. Flower
John R. Hayes
Carnegie-Mellon University

This chapter is a response to an intriguing problem. Imagine yourself faced with the following situation. A person has just arrived on the doorstep saying, "I've never written anything before; teach me how to write." Suppose then that we happened to have a model of the composing process that said that in order to write, people must perform a number of mental operations: They must Plan, Generate knowledge, Translate it into speech, and Edit what they've written. These operations can draw on information stored in long-term memory and they go on within a Task Environment that includes both the task and a growing text. In other words we have a model very similar to the one proposed in Chapter 1 of this volume.

Here then is the problem. Suppose we taught our would-be writer how to carry out each of the individual operations writers use (Planning, Generating, Translating, and Editing) just as we might teach a novice tennis player to serve, volley, and hit ground strokes. The question is: What happens when we ask our novice to put all of the pieces together, as when we place our tennis player in the middle of an actual match? What happens when people—who have this set of independent subskills—actually try to write?

This chapter attempts to use our proposed model of the writing process to describe writers in action. In other words, we would like to account, from the writer's point of view, for the *dynamics* of composing. We make two major points. The first is that the act of writing is best described as the act of juggling a number of simultaneous constraints. This is in contrast to seeing it as a series of discrete stages or steps that add up to a finished product. Second, we suggest that one of the most effective strategies for handling this large number of constraints is Planning. Plans allow writers to reduce "cognitive strain," that is, to reduce the number of demands being made on conscious attention. They also create a nested set of goals that allow a number of constraints to be satisfied at once.

In exploring the dynamics of composing, we hope to understand not only how people do it, but why they often find it difficult. This should, in turn, let us diagnose some of the problems writers encounter and suggest ways people can improve their own composing process. Let us turn first to the nature of this composing process.

Product-Based Models of Composing

There is, of course, a well-established mythology about the nature of writing as a creative process. Some of this mythology is insightful; some of it is pure bunk. Students often seem to subscribe to the inspiration paradigm in which a writer sits patiently waiting for delivery and the descent of the muse. For example, one of our subjects had just finished a writing session that looked like a wrestle with the devil; yet when we asked her to describe the normal process of a good writer, she replied that this mythical writer would "just know exactly what she wants to say. She should just know what does she want to do, or he do, um, and *just write it.*" This straightforward "think-it-say-it" model of the composing process does have a comforting simplicity. But when it is not plain wrong, it is rather useless because it tells us so little about what actually happens when people write.

An interesting contrast to the magical "think-it-say-it" model of composing is the "Pre-Write, Write, and Re-Write" model that has recently gained currency in many textbooks (Rohman, 1965). The critical assumption of Pre-Writing is that writing is a stage process; that is, the act of composition proceeds in a series of relatively discrete stages (Sommers, 1978). Pre-Writing is the stage, untouched by pen, paper, or rhetorical purpose, in which you discover your ideas. There are various avenues to this discovery. Depending on your instructor, they can range from library research, to sensory experience, to meditation and yoga. The great social value of the Pre-Writing notion is that it legitimizes thinking as a preliminary to immediate paper production. But as a model of the composing process, it still leaves the writer in the same bind; the task of writing is somehow separated from thinking, but is still unexplained.

Stage process models have little to say about the act of writing itself because they are based not on a study of the process of writing, but on the product. One suspects that they separate thinking and writing into separate stages because from the outside observer's point of view thinking and writing clearly differ: One mode creates a product whereas the other only produces troubled brows. And yet, the experience of writers rarely supports this tidy sequencing of stages. If we were to look at the composing process from the inside, we would see that the tasks of planning, retrieving information, creating new ideas, and producing and revising language all interact with one another throughout composing. A familiar example of this interaction is the way people often form their ideas through the act of putting them in writing.

A Metaphoric Process Model

If the stage process models, then, aren't convincing models of composing, is there a better way to describe the dynamics of this process? We know that when people write, they draw on a variety of mental operations such as making plans, retrieving ideas from memory, drawing inferences, creating concepts, developing an image of the reader, testing what they've written against that image, and so on. To produce any given utterance (which is to be simultaneously correct, effective, felicitous, and true), the writer must integrate a great number of these operations. The writer must exercise a number of skills and meet a number of demands—more or less all at once. As a dynamic process, writing is the act of dealing with an excessive number of simultaneous demands or constraints. Viewed this way, a writer in the act is a thinker on a full-time cognitive overload. Let us translate this notion into a composing model.

When composition texts describe writing as a series of tidy sequential steps, the role of the writer is like that of a cook baking a cake or a CPA preparing an income tax return. The writer is advised to follow certain steps: Select a topic, limit it, gather information, write it up, and then remove errors and add commas. Like the income tax procedure, this sequential process has rules or at least adages that govern the major steps, even if the act of writing is still somewhat unexplained.

The writers we have studied, however, give us a very different picture. A writer caught in the act looks much more like a very busy switchboard operator trying to juggle a number of demands on her attention and constraints on what she can do:

> She has two important calls on hold. (Don't forget that idea.)
> Four lights just started flashing. (They demand immediate attention or they'll be lost.)
> A party of five wants to be hooked up together. (They need to be connected somehow.)
> A party of two thinks they've been incorrectly connected. (Where do they go?)
> And throughout this complicated process of remembering, retrieving, and connecting, the operator's voice must project calmness, confidence, and complete control.

We use this switchboard operator as a metaphor to capture the dynamics of this process. Let us look now at the constraints themselves, which we will discuss under three broad headings: Knowledge, Written Speech, and the Rhetorical Problem.

CONSTRAINTS ON COMPOSING

To understand how constraints operate, it helps to imagine a relatively unconstrained situation—for example, one in which you could write by *simply transcribing* whatever comes to mind on the topic. Whether your task were to analyze
family relations in *Hamlet* or to write a job application, in this unconstrained
situation writing would be delightfully simple, and whatever you said would get
you an A+, an article in *PMLA*, or a new job at General Motors. By contrast
when constraints enter the picture they affect the writer in two ways: First, a
constraint is often a feature built into the writer's *goal;* therefore, any acceptable
performance will have to exhibit this feature. Second, and as a result, such
constraints actively shape the *process* of getting to a goal. For example, one of
the constraints of a United Way memo is the need to be persuasive. To meet this
goal, the writer might have to generate good arguments or subtle prods, organize
sentences for effect, and constantly monitor the tone of voice projected.
Throughout the act of writing, the rhetorical purpose would be constraining the
infinite variety of things one could say and, in the process, demanding a substantial amount of the writer's attention and effort. Therefore, constraints affect not
only *what* people write but *how* they go about doing it. Constraints take up time.

In general, the constraints an adult writer must shoulder seem to fall into three
major groups of increasing inclusiveness: the first constraint we describe as the
demand for integrated knowledge; the second is the more inclusive linguistic
conventions of written texts; and the third is the encompassing constraints of
the rhetorical problem itself. Writing is like trying to work within government
regulations from various agencies: Whatever the writer chooses to say must, in
principle, eventually conform to all of the constraints imposed from all of these
areas. Let us look at each of these kinds of constraints in more detail.

Knowledge

Generally speaking, Knowledge is a resource, not a constraint. However, it
becomes a constraint on the process when it is not in an acceptable form. In
general, expository writing calls for relatively organized, conceptually integrated
knowledge. When confronting a new or a complex issue, writers must often
move from a rich array of unorganized, perhaps even contradictory perceptions,
memories, and propositions to an integrated notion of just what it is they think
about the topic. Some writers obviously go much further down this road than
others, but much of the work of writing can be the task of transforming incoher-
ent thought and loosely related pockets of information into a highly concep-
tualized and precisely related knowledge network.

In the following protocol, we see a subject responding to the demand for
sufficiently integrated knowledge. She has probably never had to talk, much less
write, about her subject before, so her writing process is strongly constrained by
the need to formulate just what it is she thinks or knows. We see her retrieving

information from memory, drawing inferences, and relating her various ideas. We have deleted portions of the protocol that are irrelevant to this discussion; they will be shown later. There are a number of important things to notice here. If we try to diagram the writer's developing knowledge structure as a map, we find that the topography keeps changing. The writer doesn't start with a well-formed thesis that she can just develop. Instead, she must juggle her ideas around trying to decide just how they are related. "Grades" is an interesting floater. Notice how it moves about on her knowledge map.

The arrows in Fig. 2.2 indicate a general causal relationship between two ideas. If that relationship becomes further specified, the line then receives a label as in episode 3. Initially both Grades and Pressure are linked independently to Motivation (lines 1–4 in the protocol). Then Grades become identified with Pressure and subordinated to a new notion, Personal Satisfaction. In episode 3, line 9 in the protocol, Personal Satisfaction is reasserted as a cause of Motivation and the relationship between the two is further defined with the label *major*. In episodes 4 and 5, lines 15–28 in the protocol, the writer sets up a number of trial relationships in which Grades are still a subordinate element. When, however, we skip to the final draft, we find a knowledge map in which Grades and Personal Satisfaction have come to stand as independent parallel causes and each relationship has been further specified by the labels *major* and *initial*.

1. *L:* This is April, 1977, and Wendy is doing a protocol on motivation.
2. *W:* Ok, um, the issue is motivation and the problem of writing papers. For
3. me, motivation here at Carnegie-Mellon is the academic pressure and grades that
4. are involved, so I'd better put that down . . . and grades . . . Um, they kind of
5. compel me, that's really what motivation is, um, kind of to impel or start or
6. a, momentum. (Pause.) Ok, I suppose from the academic pressure of the grades,
7. I'm not sure whether—I think personal satisfaction is important, but I'm not
8. sure whether that stems from academic pressures and grades, or whether—I
9. would say personal satisfaction is a major issue. Ok, um. Oh.

14.   Not only do I get
15. satisfaction from my grades, but I also get satisfaction in turning in something
16. that is good quality. So, if I'm happy when I write a good paper, it really doesn't
17. matter what kind of grade I get back on it, if I'm happy with it. So, um, um,
18. let's see. Um, what are the—I'm thinking of, I'm trying to relate personal
19. satisfaction between academic pressure and the grades, but I'm not really sure
20. how to do it, how to branch it.

25.   Um, but
26. of course, the reason I'm writing the paper in the first place is for that grade,
27. or to relate that back. Those two ideas are very interlocked—maybe that's not
28. the right term. Um, ok.

FIG. 2.1.   Segments of a protocol.

M   MOTIVATION
P   PRESSURE
G   GRADES
PS PERSONAL SATISFACTION
Q   QUALITY

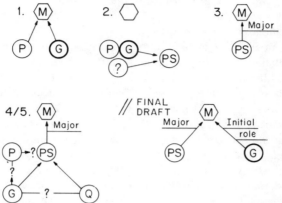

FIG. 2.2.   The writer's developing knowledge structure.

Retrieving knowledge and creating an adequate conceptual structure of "what you think" can be a demanding task. Sir Phillip Sidney's poetic advice to Astrophel, "Look into thy heart and write," is often a useful heuristic, but it doesn't guarantee that you will find a ready-made conceptual structure there.

Written Speech

If we refer to the Wendy protocol at line 11 in Fig. 2.3, we can see her trying to accommodate a second, even more demanding constraint. In addition to clarifying what she thinks, she is now trying to express that knowledge map within the linguistic and discourse conventions of written prose. Notice too how quickly she has jumped to the added task of producing text: nine lines of analysis and she is ready to set it in type.

There are many ways in which language, which enables us to express complex thought, also constrains our attempt to do it. For the inexperienced or remedial writer, the rules of grammar and conventions of usage and syntax may make an enormous demand on time and attention. But even the more experienced writer must encounter the inevitable truculence of language itself, which seems to resist our attempts to form a set of continuous sentences with forward and backward reference. A sentence that is grammatically acceptable may twist the meaning, repeat a word too soon, or have terrible rhythm. In generating a given sentence, the writer needs to meet all of these constraints more or less at once.

The following example illustrates the difference between knowing something and trying to turn that knowledge into a piece of writing. Wendy has established a knowledge map in which Motivation and Grades are related in three distinct ways. She is now trying to turn that set of thoughts into an acceptable sentence. Where we enter the protocol, she is working on the sentences that will become sentences 2, 4, and 6 in the final text.

The excerpts shown in Fig. 2.4, from Wendy's final essay and from the protocol, illustrate two interesting points:

1. Complex thoughts don't automatically flower into appropriately parallel complex sentences. Although Moliere's Bourgeois Gentleman was surprised to discover that he had been speaking "prose" all his life, doing so is no mean task. The success that sentence-combining exercises claim for improving overall writing skill (O'Hare, 1973) is probably due to their ability to reduce the effect of this linguistic constraint. By making sentence production processes somewhat more automatic, the writer has time to concentrate on other important constraints.

2. In addition to producing a verbal rendition of thought, our writer must also

1. *L:* This is April, 1977, and Wendy is doing a protocol on motivation.
2. *W:* Ok, um, the issue is motivation and the problem of writing papers. For
3. me, motivation here at Carnegie-Mellon is the academic pressure and grades that
4. are involved, so I'd better put that down . . . and grades . . . Um, they kind of
5. compel me, that's really what motivation is, um, kind of to impel or start or
6. a, momentum. (Pause.) Ok, I suppose from the academic pressure of the grades,
7. I'm not sure whether—I think personal satisfaction is important, but I'm not
8. sure whether that stems from academic pressures and grades, or whether—I
9. would say personal satisfaction is a major issue. Ok, um. Oh.
10. *L:* What are you thinking?
11. *W:* I'm trying to think of the first sentence to start with. Um, maybe something
12. like, personal satisfaction is the major motivating force in the writing of my
13. papers and reports. Ok, I'm trying to think of—ok, I want to somehow get it into
14. the academic pressures now. Um, well, maybe not so soon. Ok. Not only do I get
15. satisfaction from my grades, but I also get satisfaction in turning in something
16. that is good quality. So, if I'm happy when I write a good paper, it really doesn't
17. matter what kind of grade I get back on it, if I'm happy with it. So, um, um,
18. let's see. Um, what are the—I'm thinking of, I'm trying to relate personal
19. satisfaction between academic pressure and the grades, but I'm not really sure
20. how to do it, how to branch it. I'm really having a hard time getting started.
21. Well, maybe I'll just write a bunch of ideas down, and maybe try to connect them after
22. I finish. Ok. When I feel that I've written a high quality, and I put in paren-
23. theses, professional, paper, um, to be graded, when I submit it, the grade is not
24. always necessary for the teacher to have the same. Ok, that's kind of _____
25. _____; I'll check with that one. Ok, and—Let's see what else. Um, but
26. of course, the reason I'm writing the paper in the first place is for that grade,
27. or to relate that back. Those two ideas are very interlocked—maybe that's not
28. the right term. Um, ok. I'm not always sure whether my personal satisfaction,
29. this is kind of off on a tangent, and it might not be included in my final draft,

FIG. 2.3.   Wendy protocol.

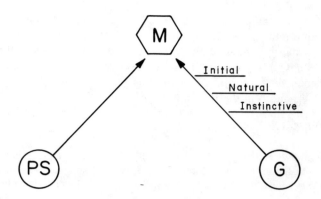

Sentences from Final Version:

2. Because of the emphasis on 4.0s here at CMU, grades become an instinctive motivator for myself.

4. The initial motivator in the outset of writing a paper is the fact that a grade will be attached to it upon completion.

6. After I begin writing a paper, the grade emphasis diminishes and a higher level of personal satisfaction takes over.

Protocol Excerpt:

Um, because of the, maybe because of the emphasis—Um, 4.0's. Trying to be more specific. Um, even though I don't have a 4.0. Um, because of the emphasis on 4.0's. Ok, because of the emphasis on 4.0's, grades are maybe a natural, or maybe instinctive, are instinctive motivator.

So um, ok. The *initial* motivator, this is, grades are *natural instinctive* motivator, —I should say *initially* again, but I'm not really sure how to say it. Ok, maybe I can leave it *natural*, or *instinctive*—maybe that'll bring that out. Um, ok, maybe I can refer toward *initially* again. After the um, after I begin perhaps, writing. Ah, a paper, the fact that a grade, wait a minute, the fact that a grade, I don't know if I used later, attached—oh, I did, I don't want to use that again. Ok, um.

After I begin writing a paper, the grade emphasis—I don't know if I want to use that again—the grade emphasis is foreshadowed by the, by the fact or maybe I'll come back and put that in . . . oh, ok. After I begin writing a paper the grade emphasis is foreshadowed by the something, um, something that instead,— I'll have to look up the wording.

FIG. 2.4.   Turning thoughts into acceptable sentences.

work within the conventions of written speech, particularly those conventions that distinguish oral speech from writing and make writing a specialized form of discourse. Even from this brief protocol passage, we can infer that the writer probably has a set of rules or adages about paper writing that say:

    a. Be specific.

    b. Repeat ideas for emphasis.

    c. Refer back for coherence.

d. Don't repeat words/phrases in close proximity.
e. Use "correct" (?) wording.

Turning verbal thought into text is a demanding task. Mina Shaughnessy's work with Basic Writers (1977) has shown that many of their writing errors come from a misapplication of oral speech conventions to writing. Other writers have suggested that although written speech is a specialized and difficult convention to master, it is the language of modern education. In particular, David Olson and E. D. Hirsch have recently described the difference between an *utterance* and a *text* in terms of our expectations that a *text* will be fully contextualized (Hirsch, 1977; Olson, 1977). In other words, we expect that the meaning in written speech will be fully contained and explicitly present in the text itself—as it never is in oral speech. By contrast, the meaning of an *utterance* often depends in large part on a context shared by speaker and listener, on the immediate situation, shared intentions, prior knowledge, and, of course, on many forms of paralanguage—tone, emphasis, and body language. To compensate for all that lost contextual meaning, the writer of a *text* must draw on the specialized conventions of written discourse in order to contextualize the meaning. A writer is not simply expressing herself or himself but is creating a peculiar kind of artifact.

Hirsch (1977) sums up this position in describing two sets of such conventions:

1. The scribal, lexical, and syntactic conventions of the normative written dialect: what we generally call the "basic" skills.
2. The stylistic conventions which make it possible to communicate with a large, distant, and diverse readership by providing expectations, frequent closure, and an adequate context for statements.

Olson (1977) and Hirsch (1977) have described some of the constraints imposed by written speech by a study of the text itself. However, this constraint of "text-making" also affects the writer's process. One of the important things protocol analysis reveals is that a great part of skill in writing is the ability to monitor and direct one's own composing process. This, we think, will be a valuable and fascinating area for research, but one that we can only touch on here. As you could see in the protocol (Fig. 2.3), Wendy had to decide how to get started, what to do next, and how to keep track of where she had been and where she wanted to go. Handling the very process of composing itself is a demanding and, no doubt, learned procedure. Some writers have a large and powerful repertory of composing skills; others don't. For example, not all of our subjects are able to tell themselves to jot down ideas and connect them later when it would be quite useful to do so. They seem to lack this degree of conscious control over the process of writing itself.

To sum up then, the linguistic conventions of written speech constrain writers in two important ways. Not only must they learn many conventions peculiar to written speech, they must learn how to handle the rather long and complicated process of composing itself. Our subjects have already shown us that there are significant differences between writers in their organization and control of the composing process.

Rhetorical Problem

Finally, the task of writing is complicated by one last and very large constraint: the demands of the rhetorical problem. Whatever writers choose to say must ultimately conform to the structures posed by their *purpose* in writing, their sense of the *audience,* and their *projected selves* or imagined roles. In essence, writing is also a speech act and therefore subject to all the constraints of any interpersonal performance.

In practice this means that writers must adapt both knowledge and written speech to solving this rhetorical problem. For some writers, this is the straw that breaks the camel's back. Although the Rhetorical Problem is an added constraint, it can't conveniently be "added" at the end, because, in theory, it should direct the entire process of generating knowledge and language.

JUGGLING CONSTRAINTS

Having described some of the constraints of writing, let us look at how people deal with them. It is no wonder that many find writing difficult. It is the very nature of the beast to impose a large set of converging but potentially contradictory constraints on the writer. Furthermore, to be efficient the writer should attend to all of these constraints at once; when all is said and done they must be integrated. One doesn't, for example, generate all of one's knowledge on a topic and then decide what to do with it. Ideally, each utterance a writer generates would be at once perfectly accurate, well-formed itself, integrated in the text, and rhetorically effective. Unfortunately, this ideal rarely occurs because of the limited number of items our short-term memory or conscious attention can handle. Humans are basically serial processors and not well adapted to handling a large number of simultaneous demands on attention (Newell & Simon, 1972). This means that we must handle converging constraints by juggling them in clever ways. The remainder of this chapter looks at some of the important strategies writers use to deal with the problem.

The use of strategy in writing is analogous to the use of strategy in concept attainment. In *A Study of Thinking,* Bruner, Goodnow, and Austin (1956) described strategy as a "pattern of decisions" taken to meet certain objectives [p. 54]. In both cases the writer/thinker is trying to reduce what Bruner et al. called "cognitive strain," that is, the demand placed on short-term memory or conscious attention. In various ways each strategy we describe will either decrease the number of constraints being acted on or it will lower the level at which they are deemed satisfied. The catch is that some strategies that are very effective at reducing "cognitive strain" are not particularly effective at producing good writing.

Strategies for Reducing Constraints

In theory the most obvious solution to the problem of excessive constraints is to divide writing into temporarily independent stages such as Pre-Write, Write, and Re-Write, or Gather Information, Outline, Write, and Edit. But in practice this solution often violates the very nature of writing that demands integration of all these elements. Perhaps that is why the writers we have studied don't work in this way, but appear to depend on other strategies to reduce constraints.

Throw a Constraint Away.   When a juggler has too many balls to keep in the air, the easiest solution is to simply toss one out over her shoulder. Writers can do this too, for example, by simply choosing to ignore their audience or the convention that demands coherence between paragraphs.

Partition the Problem.   One powerful problem-solving strategy is to break a large complex problem down into semi-independent subproblems. Writers do this in a general way when they plan to write and revise. However, within the act of composing itself, writers often depend on a shifting, selective focus of attention. Like the shifting focus of a moving spotlight, a writer might alternate between simply generating ideas and then testing them against an imagined reader.

In teaching composition, the argument for heuristics (Flower & Hayes, 1977) and especially for invention procedures (Young, Becker, & Pike, 1970) rests on the notion that by partitioning a problem you reduce the number of constraints active at one time, and second, that by concentrating on a subtask you do the task more effectively. However, a word of caution is in order. The kind of partitioning we are describing here should not be confused with the notion of stages in the composing process. Mental operations such as Generating or Editing can be done independently, but within the act of composing they occur in interactive, recursive patterns, not stages.

Although partitioning is a powerful strategy, it raises a question: How do the pieces get reintegrated? Obviously, a strategy such as write and revise, which simply ignores some constraints until later, will work better for lower level concerns such as correct spelling. But partitioning alone will not be enough to deal with such integral constraints as achieving a rhetorical purpose.

Set Priorities and "Satisfice."   Writing is a complex task. That Platonic entity, "good writing," has so many possible features, from truth telling to tone control, that a writer must generally choose which goals to achieve at what level of success. Writers inevitably set such priorities in the way they define their Rhetorical Problem (e.g., this is a letter to Aunt Tilly, so you can safely ignore run-on sentences and fragments; she won't mind). In setting certain priorities (e.g., be friendly and write at least two pages), writers in effect eliminate some other constraints or reduce the level at which they will be deemed satisfied.

Although setting priorities works to diminish the problem and reduce cognitive strain, it would be foolish to treat the strategy itself as a rational or even purely "cognitive" decision. As Britton, Burgess, Martin, McLeod, & Rosen (1975) have described, many affective concerns shape the writer's priorities and his or her definition of the task (e.g., see if you can write three pages that won't get any red marks this time). A writer's motivation and self-confidence can dictate a definition of acceptability that might be only loosely tied to his or her actual ability.

In school, "bad writing" is often the name we apply to writing whose priorities we feel to be askew. For example, the "theme writing" criticized by Coles and others (Coles, 1974) is a student genre characterized by a facile use of inflated language and a concern for correctness at the expense of honesty, emotion, and imagination.

As a corollary to giving some constraints a high priority, writers then choose to "satisfice" on others (Newell & Simon, 1972). A writer "satisfices" by choosing to take the first acceptable solution. For instance, instead of struggling to find the "best" way to say something, the writer satisfices with the first "acceptable" sentence and moves on to other matters. Writers often combine this strategy with partitioning when they decide to satisfice on certain things in a first draft and improve them in revision. A side effect of satisficing, which we see in techniques like brainstorming, is that in reducing the cognitive task, it also reduces a writer's performance anxiety. This in turn frees more of the writer's attention for the real problems.

Draw on a Routine or Well-Learned Procedure.   One way to reduce cognitive strain is to depend on procedures that are so automatized or routine that they don't require conscious processing in Short-Term Memory. For example, experienced writers usually devote very little conscious attention to tasks such as typing, producing grammatical sentences, or even meeting the demands of a particular genre, whereas these tasks can overwhelm inexperienced writers. Even some very high-level tasks can be treated as routine if the writer has a stored frame or schema in memory to draw on. For example, the conventional frame for the outraged, solid citizen's letter to the editor could make such a letter relatively easy for most of us to write. It specifies not only the writer's role, tone of voice, and a set of stock phrases ("This injustice should not be allowed to continue!"); it also supplies at least a skeletal rhetorical structure and a declamatory sentence style.

Drawing on routine procedures or stored frames is a powerful strategy because of its great cognitive economy. Learning how to write is, in part, the process of making certain subtasks so automatic that we open up processing space in short-term memory and increase our capacity to deal with those harder tasks that require conscious attention (Nold, in press). The limitation of the strategy is, of course, its inflexibility. A stereotypic plan is only effective when it meets the appropriate stereotypic situation.

Plan.   If excessive constraints have been the villain of this piece, Plans are most likely to be its hero because planning can not only reduce constraints, but can integrate them. As an important strategy in all kinds of problem-solving activity, Plans tend to work in three ways: by modeling, abstraction, and analogy (Hayes, 1978). An outline, for example, is essentially a miniature model of the proposed solution. A model, of course, is much cheaper to build than the full-sized solution would be, if, for example, the goal were a battleship or a 20-page paper. The model lets the writer (1) define manageable subproblems and (2) test and discard alternatives. However, if the model is not cheap to build—if it is a 5-page typed outline—the writer may be very reluctant to discard his plan whether it is good or not. In the early stages of writing, it is important to use plans that are detailed enough to test, but cheap enough to throw away.

Planning also works by abstracting the essential features from something complex (Miller, Galanter & Pribram, 1960). Plans reduce a large unwieldy problem loaded with constraints—such as, write a perfect paper—down to a simpler one—jot down your main ideas. Such plans are like a designer's sketch: They focus on the essentials; they set priorities. By setting priorities, plans also tell you how to go about solving the problem. For example, the designer's plan or sketch for a new garden will probably include only the major elements, the plots, the paths, and the existing trees, but will probably exclude individual dandelions and transient insects. Just so, a writer's plan isolates key issues and goals out of that tide of details and language that often sweeps writers away before it. Plans are, in a sense, the writer's defense against the very nature of writing and its deluge of constraints. They offer a touchstone or a steady reference point in one's effort to create sentences and a text. By contrast, some writers often try to figure out their ideas and goals by trying to write a perfect introductory paragraph.

Plans can of course be elaborate, detailed, and formal, but the most useful plans we have seen appear to be the sketchy flexible sort that recognizes priorities and defines the writer's high-level goals. As the writer works, a sketchy plan (such as, try to present ballet to teenage boys as a form of athletic skill) becomes fleshed out in close interaction with the act of generating and organizing ideas. Good plans appear to be like an artist's sketch in which the essentials are suggested but implicit in the movement of a line. Again, good plans are rich enough to work from and argue about, but cheap enough to throw away.

Planning has another virtue; it is a highly teachable strategy. In trying to bridge theory and practice, we are going to describe three kinds of plans writers make and teachers might teach. In making this jump from analysis to teaching it might be useful to review where we have been. Our argument so far has been basically this: Contrary to some traditional notions, the writing process is not a neat, additive sequence of stages. Instead, the task of the writer is better described as an attempt to juggle three sets of constraints, all of which should impinge on the final product. The writer's problem then is how to keep all of these balls in the air given the limits of our short-term memory—our capacity to juggle.

One of the most effective strategies for reducing cognitive strain without ignoring interacting constraints is planning. Therefore, it is no surprise that in the writers we have studied, planning takes up a good deal of the time spent composing. Furthermore, good writers appear to have more flexible, high-level plans and more self-conscious control of their planning than poor writers (Flower & Hayes, in press). It is our thesis that one way to improve people's writing is to improve the planning process they go through *as they write*.

A Taxonomy of Writing Plans

We know that writers generate an enormous number and variety of plans as they compose; the problem is how to categorize these plans in a useful way. Our hypothesis is that writers draw on three major kinds of plans which are hierarchically related to one another.

Plans to Do

To begin with, writers generate plans for dealing with their Rhetorical Problem. These rhetorical plans are called plans *To Do* something in or by language. These are essentially plans for performing a speech act—for responding in some way to that rhetorical problem, which includes the writer, the reader, and a purpose. A plan *To Do* something in writing might be as unique and specific as "Write a note for the icebox door to keep the family out of the plums. Use a stern

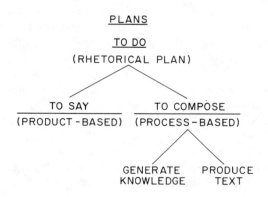

FIG. 2.5. Plan for dealing with a Rhetorical Problem.

parental voice that begins with firm reasonableness and ends with a veiled threat.'" At the other extreme a rhetorical plan could be as conventional and limited as "write another essay for Freshman Composition class." As you might expect when writers fail to plan or depend on limited, stereotypic plans, they are likely to spend very little time actively considering audience or purpose when they write. They are more likely to produce "Writer-Based prose," which takes on the structure of the writer's own thought process and the style of an interior monologue (Flower, 1979).

A rhetorical plan To Do something can not only improve the quality of a paper; it can also make it easier to write. When people treat writing as a speech act, they are more likely to draw on many of the well-learned strategies adults use everyday for arguing, explaining, or describing, but which many seem to ignore when they are writing for a class. A rhetorical plan offers the writer a pole star for the choppy sea of trying to compose.

How can we help students to make vigorous plans To Do something? A recent study by Scardamalia, Bracewell, and Bereiter (1978) suggests that assignments that specify a particular audience in some detail act as important cues to writers. They help them "decenter" from their content or information and adapt their knowledge to a reader.

If you want to get better writing from your students, one of the most effective ways to do it is to create assignments that have a realistic purpose and a real audience (not a teacher), who actually needs to know something. For example, one can request a written plan from students 2 weeks in advance in which they identify the reader and his needs, their role vis-á-vis that reader, and the impact they expect their paper to have. Many times this plan can become the problem-purpose statement that introduces the paper.

Plans to Say

In order to carry out a plan To Do something, writers often generate two kinds of subplans. The first of these is the familiar and rudimentary plan that all schoolchildren have had drilled into them in the form of outlining: a plan for what you want *To Say*. A plan To Say something is essentially a content plan—a simplified or abstract version of the information you want to convey. It can take a variety of forms, ranging from scribbled notes and sketches on an envelope to an impressive sentence outline complete with Roman numerals and two subpoints under every point. A plan To Say is essentially a scale model of the final product. Perhaps that is why it has been so widely and rigorously taught, often to the exclusion of any other kind of planning.

Composing Plans

There is, however, another kind of planning writers do that is based not on the product of writing, but on the process. This third kind of plan we call a Composing Plan.

Some Composing Plans help people generate knowledge. In classical rhetoric, such formalized plans go under the name of invention. One can choose from highly systematic and analytical plans, such as the particle, wave, field analysis of tagmemics, to Aristotle's topics or Gordon's synectics. Or one could choose from more enigmatic and inspirational plans, such as Sheridan Baker's (1969) advice on "picking an argument" or the meditation techniques used in Pre-Writing, on down to the time-honored methods of poetic inspiration, "Look into your heart and write." If you wish your students to have more self-conscious control over the process of generating ideas, there are many ways to teach it.

The category of Composing Plans also includes a large set of ad hoc plans people use to guide themselves through the process of writing. For example, when the writer in the Wendy protocol ran into trouble, she told herself to "write a bunch of ideas down and connect them later." Some of our subjects appear to be at the mercy of inspiration as they compose, or slaves to their own growing text. Others are able not only to monitor their composing process, but to choose alternative ways to proceed. At the base of our work with heuristic strategies for writers (Flower & Hayes, 1977) is an attempt to learn more about these unexplored alternative strategies within the art of composing itself.

Let us close with an excerpt from a protocol that illustrates a writer working under a top-level plan To Do something, which in turn creates a nested set of goals and subgoals. As the protocol develops, we see how the writer's forward progress is the result of a recursive, nonlinear process guided by a variety of plans. As an illuminating contrast to this Subject, we studied another writer whom we shall call "Freewrite." As he composed, Freewrite's top-level plan appeared to be "Write whatever comes to mind." His guiding plan was essentially a plan To Say, with only a rudimentary set of composing rules tacked on (e.g., use correct grammar, use correct spelling if you know it, and paragraph occasionally). His protocol showed almost no discernable attention given to audience or purpose, and the final product, as you might guess, read rather like a transcript of free association, even though the writer considered it quite adequate.

We return then to the writer working under a top-level plan To Do. This schematic version of a protocol covers the beginning of the composing session. The plans To Do and To Compose are generally comments the writer makes to himself, whereas the plans To Say are frequently notes jotted on paper. Notice how the first three moves essentially define the rhetorical problem.

By move 4, the writer has sketched out the rhetorical problem (his purpose, audience, and his own role) and set up a composing plan (just jot things down). When he begins to explore his knowledge at move 4, it is under the simultaneous control of these two plans.

Move 5, a decision to keep on generating ideas, is a reaffirmation and development of the initial composing plan in Move 2.

By move 7, the information the writer has generated leads him to form a new

PLANS:	TO DO	TO COMPOSE	TO SAY
1.	Write an exposition for humanities teachers about Memory I (a group of specialized memory techniques).		
2.		What I'll do is jot down random thoughts about	
3.	What the teachers might want to hear and I might want to to tell them.		
4.			First thing that occurs randomly is encoding.
5.		That word means a lot but I won't explain it now.	
6.			Thinking about objections heard at the workshop. Rote memory is trivial.
7.		A point I will want to make someplace is that	
8.			Memory I procedures are useful in modern language. They are also more useful generally. Unfortunately, by more generally I mean things like grocery lists.
9.	One of the problems in writing this essay will be to expand on that usefulness and make it seem more plausible. To make uses more general and acceptable. That's the wrong word; I mean important seeming. Uh. Or, if that's		

(*continued*)

PLANS:	TO DO	TO COMPOSE	TO SAY
	not the solution to the problem, alternate approach is to say		
10.			so those applications aren't important. What is important is the instructional value
11.		Not the right word but what the hell	
12.			of the demonstration of encoding

FIG. 2.6.   Excerpt from a protocol: Working by plan.

plan that is both a Composing plan for the final paper and a plan To Do something—to make a point for the reader.

Move 9 is probably the most illuminating point of the protocol because the writer encounters a mismatch between his Knowledge (things he could say about Memory I) and his goal vis-á-vis the reader. His action demonstrates the distinction between Knowledge and Goals in writing. His high-level plan To Do, based on his purpose and reader, lets him consider two subplans (make the subject itself important or focus on its underlying principle) and in turn two pockets of knowledge. In the process of working by plan our writer considers two radically different things he could say. Clearly his writing process is not simply the straightforward act of expressing what he knows. Instead it is a hierarchically organized, recursive process in which knowledge and text are generated under the direction of both a rhetorical plan To Do something and a Composing plan for how to do it in writing.

This fragment of protocol was the beginning of the Subject's writing session. At the end of the session, 40 minutes later, there was an unexpected coda: The writer discovered that his initial objective of "justifying Memory I" had been entirely forgotten in the course of composing a different line of argument. He now sees that Memory I (and the ideas generated in our excerpt) could be an example in this larger argument. In the following brief section, he sets up a new plan (which is both a rhetorical and a composing plan) and begins to compose text.

This excerpt illustrates what is probably one of the critical differences we have seen between the processes of good and weak writers. Weak writers in this situation would probably continue to crunch out text under the direction of a plan To Say what they knew or a plan To Compose their information into "acceptable" text. Good writers, by contrast, not only make initial high-level plans To Do something, but continue to return to and develop those plans as they write.

PLANS:	TO DO	TO COMPOSE	TO SAY
1.	If we were to describe Memory I (as an example) what do we want to say about? (Searches notes) There it is. Let's do that.		
2.		All right, *I will take/take as an example of the sorts of material . . . presented in the course* . . . Now this is a terrible sentence but we can revise it. *. . . the first subunit of . . . unit . . . unit.* That's not quite right, but, *called Memory I. In Memory I, Memory I . . . In Memory I the students learn* . . . Now what am I going to do here cause I don't really have an organization for Memory I yet. *. . . the students learn* . . . Now at this point we should break off and plan.	
3.	Let's see . . . now what we want to get across in this plan, we want to illustrate the practical nature . . . nature of skills.		

Note: Lines in italics are fragments of the growing text interrupted by plans and meta comments.

FIG. 2.7. Protocol of the beginning of a writing session.

In applying this discussion of planning to teaching, one thing stands out. Outlining—that old warhorse of composition teaching—can fail to help students if it only encourages them to plan what they want To Say—that is, to record and organize information. Outlining, and in fact any technique for organizing ideas, can be a powerful tool. But perhaps we have concentrated too long on teaching plans To Say at the expense of the other kinds of plans writers also need to make. As we all know, in effective writing a meaningful organization of information takes its logic from the writer's higher level plan To Do something. Perhaps we need to teach such plans more vigorously. Second, even if writers know what they want to accomplish and what to say, they must still face the task of trying to compose. Good writers have plans and strategies for handling this task. One of the current tasks of rhetoric is to explore and explain those skills that govern how we write.

REFERENCES

Baker, S. *The practical stylist*. New York: Thomas Crowell, 1969.

Britton, J., Burgess, T., Martin, N., McLeod, A., & Rosen, H. *The development of writing abilities (11-18)*. London: MacMillan, 1975.

Bruner, J., Goodnow, J., & Austin, G. *A study of thinking*. New York: Wiley, 1956.

Coles, W. *Teaching composing: Writing as a self-creating process* (teacher's edition). Rochelle Park, N.J.: Hayden, 1974.

Flower, L. *Writer based prose: A cognitive basis for problems in writing*. Manuscript in preparation, 1979.

Flower, L., & Hayes, J. R. Problem-solving strategies and the writing process. *College English*, 1977, *39*, 449–461.

Flower, L., & Hayes, J. R. Plans and the cognitive process of composing. In C. Frederiksen, M. Whiteman, & J. Dominic (Eds.), *Writing: The nature, development and teaching of written communication*. Hillsdale, N.J.: Lawrence Erlbaum Associates, in press.

Hayes, J. R. *Cognitive psychology: Thinking and creating*. Homewood, Ill.: Dorsey, 1978.

Hirsch, E. D. *The philosophy of composition*. Chicago: University of Chicago Press, 1977.

Miller, G., Galanter, E., & Pribram, K. *Plans and the structure of behavior*. New York: Holt, Rinehart & Winston, 1960.

Newell, A., & Simon, H. *Human problem solving*. Englewood Cliffs, N.J.: Prentice-Hall, 1972.

Nold, E. Revising. In C. Frederiksen, M. Whiteman, & J. Dominic (Eds.), *Writing: The nature, development and teaching of written communication*. Hillsdale, N.J.: Lawrence Erlbaum Associates, in press.

O'Hare, F. *Sentence-combining: Improving student writing without formal grammar instruction*. Urbana, Ill.: National Council of Teachers of English, 1973.

Olson, D. From utterance to text: The bias of language in speech and writing. *The Harvard Educational Review*, 1977, *47*(3), 257–281.

Rohman, G. Pre-writing: The stage of discovery in the writing process. *College Composition and Communication*, 1965, *16*, 106–112.

Scardamalia, M., Bracewell, R., & Bereiter, C. *Writing and decentered thought: The development of audience awareness*. Paper presented at American Educational Research Association, Toronto, Canada, March 1978.

Shaughnessy, M. *Errors and expectations*. New York: Oxford, 1977.

Sommers, N. Response to Sharon Crowley, "Components of the composing process." *College Composition and Communication*, 1978, *29*, 209–211.

Young, R., Becker, A., & Pike, K. *Rhetoric: Discovery and change*. New York: Harcourt, Brace & World, 1970.

3 A Framework for a Cognitive Theory of Writing

Allan Collins
Dedre Gentner
Bolt Beranek and Newman Inc.

INTRODUCTION

A major breakthrough in the teaching of writing has been made possible by the convergence of two recent developments in science and technology. Cognitive science, which brings together the disciplines of cognitive psychology, artificial intelligence, and linguistics, has begun to provide us with the theoretical means for constructing formal process theories of human cognition. Thus we now have many of the tools needed for constructing a process theory of writing. At the same time, technology is being developed to manipulate and edit text. Soon this technology will be relatively inexpensive and commonplace. It should be possible to merge these two developments into a computer-based ''Writing Land'' for teaching and assisting people in writing. This would be an environment with writing tasks and games that can provide the basis for a computer-based writing curriculum.

The Status of a Theory of Writing

It is our view that it is possible and worthwhile to develop a theory of the writing process that can incorporate some of the insights of artists and rhetoricians, but that is precise enough to be testable, at least in part. Early theories of writing will undoubtedly prove to be both wrong and incomplete, but, by conducting psychological experiments, such as those described by Bereiter, Flower, Hayes, or Gould in this volume, we can discover which parts of the theory are correct and which parts need to be refined or replaced.

A second advantage of a precise theory is the possibility of embedding it in computer technology. Anything less than a carefully detailed theory will not suffice. For example, if a theory of editing does not specify all the necessary conditions for making a certain change, then the advice such a system would give would often be inappropriate and annoying. But by attempting to implement a theory on a computer, another kind of scientific refinement process is initiated. As we see what kinds of inappropriate or wrong advice are given, we can correct the theory so that it does not lead to such mistakes. Thus, through computer implementation and psychological testing, we can refine the initial theory of writing and achieve a more sophisticated understanding of the writing process.

Another question that arises is whether a theory of writing should concern how writing ought to be done or how writing *is* done; that is, should we aim for a prescriptive theory or a descriptive theory? Our feeling is that both are needed, and further, that our prescriptive theory must be illuminated by our descriptive knowledge so that our views of how things ought to be done are compatible with human propensities.

In the following section, we have tried to indicate the kinds of rules and processes we see as belonging in a theory of writing. But the goal of a complete theory is rather far away. We have only started working toward it.

Elements of a Theory of Writing

The kind of theory we envision views writing as a process of generating and editing text within a variety of constraints. The constraints come from three sources: *structure* (what are good sentence forms, paragraph forms, and text forms), *content* (what ideas are to be expressed and how are they related), and *purpose* (what are the goals of the writer and what is his or her model of the reader). Trying to satisfy all these constraints at one time is what makes writing difficult and what often leads to "writing block" in adults and children.

At the highest level, the writing process can be separated into *producing ideas* and *producing text* for those ideas. The major categories of producing ideas and producing text can be further separated into component subprocesses, as we show later. Teaching people to separate the various task components allows them to learn how to use the most effective generation strategies for each subprocess, how to edit with respect to each subprocess, and how to ignore other constraints while working on a subprocess (Flower & Hayes, in press). People who write a lot develop many of these techniques, which unfortunately are not usually taught explicitly and must be learned in a painful trial-and-error fashion.

Equally important for a theory of writing is a theory of the text-structure constraints operating in fluent writing. Such a theory would be a theory of *good* structures as opposed to a theory of *well-formed* structures. Most formal theories heretofore have concentrated on defining well-formedness. For example, a syntactic grammar attempts to specify the set of well-formed sentences (e.g., Chomsky, 1957) and a story grammar attempts to specify the set of well-formed stories (e.g., Rumelhart, 1975). But books on how to write (Hall, 1973; Strunk

& White, 1972) specify a different class of constraints on sentence, paragraph, and text structures, constraints designed to make texts more readable. The *good* structures fitting these constraints are in general a subset of the set of well-formed structures. We think it is possible to develop a linguistic theory of good structures for sentences, paragraphs, and texts, but it requires a new kind of linguistic analysis. Such a theory would have direct implications for the teaching of writing.

Finally, a theory of writing should provide a description of where the major difficulties arise in the process. In particular, the theory should allow a fairly precise characterization of the problems most often experienced by beginning writers, as well as some techniques for surmounting these problems.

In the main sections of this chapter, we discuss the two major subprocesses in writing, idea production and text production. Then we briefly discuss why writing is so difficult to learn. Finally, we present our speculations on "Writing Land."

IDEA PRODUCTION

It is important to separate idea production from text production. The processes involved in producing text, whether they operate on the word level, the sentence level, the paragraph level, or the text level, must produce a linear sequence that satisfies certain grammatical rules. In contrast, the result of the process of idea production is a set of ideas with many internal connections, only a few of which may fit the linear model desirable for text. Although the set of ideas generated is subject to rules of logical consistency, plausibility, and relevance, these rules are traditionally less codified than the rules for text production, and the number of allowable relationships between ideas is greater than the number of allowable relationships between elements of text. This difference is reflected in the fact that advice given for idea production usually has a free-style quality to it: People are advised to brainstorm or to use adventurous thinking (Bartlett, 1932; Flower & Hayes, in press).

The importance of the distinction between producing ideas and producing text cannot be overemphasized. As Flower and Hayes (in press), Wason (1965), and others have pointed out, one of the most damaging habits for a novice writer to have is that of confusing idea manipulation with text manipulation so that text structure constraints enter into the process of writing at an early stage, before the ideas are ready. When this happens, not only does the writer waste a great deal of time and effort polishing prose that will eventually be discarded, but, even worse, the effort to perfect text may cause the writer to lose track of the desired content. Part of the reason that novice writers have difficulty accepting the distinction between idea production and text production is that it is very unintuitive to realize the degree to which one's own ideas can be opaque, inaccessible, self-contradictory, and in other ways in need of considerable strategic management in order to emerge as the clear, well-reasoned positions we believe we have. Only experience can really convince someone of the astonishing paradox that we can in some sense have an idea but not be able to find it, and that, once the idea is found, we may decide to reject it. Because these notions are not obvious, it is important that educators make such distinctions explicit when teaching novice writers.

At least two different subprocesses are involved in idea production: capturing ideas and manipulating ideas. The names for these subprocesses are arbitrary, but they help to delineate the subprocesses. These subprocesses are generally interleaved in most people's writing, but in some situations it is possible to separate them and to apply systematic generation and editing strategies for each process. This kind of separation is most important for the beginning writer. The strategies we describe are most effective for expository writing, but they can also be applied to creative writing.

Capturing Ideas

One of the simplest, yet most effective things to do if you want to write on a given topic is to write down all the ideas you have that are related to the topic. It is important to do this before imposing an elegant text structure in order not to limit the ideas you will discover (Flower & Hayes, in press).

Other systematic strategies for finding ideas include:

1. Keeping a journal of interesting ideas and events.
2. Brainstorming with a group.
3. Looking in books (source materials).
4. Getting suggestions from somebody.
5. Trying to explain your ideas to somebody.

Essential to all these strategies is getting the ideas down in tangible form so that they can be grouped, manipulated, and altered.

Interestingly enough it often turns out that even when writers believe that they already have a number of ideas on a given topic, the process of idea capturing will reveal that there are more ideas than were realized at first. Also, getting the ideas down in rough but tangible form paves the way for the stage of idea-manipulation, in which new ideas may be discovered and some old ideas may be rejected.

Manipulating Ideas

The line between manipulating old ideas and inventing new ideas is difficult to draw. We do not attempt to make a distinction here but instead describe strategies for manipulating ideas that often end up leading to new ideas. Most people intuitively invoke many of these strategies but they seldom apply them systematically. We think it is useful to try to specify all of these strategies and to delineate how they are applied most effectively. We briefly describe the strategies we have enumerated so far. To illustrate them, we show how they could be applied to the problem of describing a particular party one went to. The strategies are specified in terms of an object, event, or concept x under consideration:

1. Identifying Dependent Variable(s).   The first thing to do is to determine what are the interesting or relevant aspects of the concept to focus on as dependent variables. In the case of a party, one might chose to focus on how interesting (or boring) the party was.

2. Critical-Case Generation.   The strategy is to generate critical cases for comparison with x. The critical cases should be as diverse as possible so as to vary on all possible dimensions that are relevant to evaluating the dependent variable. For example, one wants to consider small and large parties, parties with friends or strangers, parties with or without alcohol or food, and particularly unusual parties.

3. Compare to Similar Cases (Analogize).   When a similarity is found on the dependent variable between two cases, or between two conceptual domains, it is useful to compare the two cases to identify any other properties that are similar and that might account for the similarity of the two cases on the dependent variable. This mapping over cases or domains is often referred to as metaphor or analogy (Gentner, 1977a, 1977b). For the purposes of teasing out underlying factors, the more dissimilar the two domains that are compared, the more likely will any similarities identified be relevant to accounting for the similarity between the domains on the dependent variable. Although the initial metaphorical insight is often an overall feeling of similarity, it can usually be pushed to lead to a set of more detailed correspondences. Finding, or failing to find, any of these correspondences can lead to new ideas.

In the example of an interesting party, the strategy is to compare it to other interesting events or objects in order to identify the properties they have in common that might account for their being interesting. For example, by considering other interesting parties, one might decide that there is an optimal balance between old friends and strangers, that alcohol is practically always served, etc. By considering interesting books, one might decide that interestingness derives from fast pacing and psychological twists and turns. The more dissimilar the events and objects compared, the more likely that their commonalities can account for their interestingness.

4. Compare to Dissimilar Cases (Contrast or Differentiate).   When a difference is found between two cases or conceptual domains on the dependent variable, a good strategy for generating new ideas is to look for factors to explain the difference. For example, in earlier work (Collins, Warnock, Aiello, & Miller, 1975) one of our respondents, when faced with explaining why China had high population density and Siberia did not, constructed an explanation that the cold climate in Siberia leads people to die of exposure. He constructed this hypothesis from knowledge about the difference in climate between the two places, knowledge that people sometimes die of exposure to cold, and knowledge that death lowers population. This example illustrates how people use differentiation to construct new ideas based on their prior knowledge. For the purposes of teasing out differences, the more similar the two domains that are compared, the more likely will any differences identified be relevant to accounting for the difference between the domains on the dependent variable. This is the notion of the "minimal pair" in linguistics (cf. Gleason, 1961) or the "near miss" in artificial intelligence (cf. Winston, 1977).

In the party example, one may want to compare parties that missed being interesting for some reason or other. For example, at one there may have been silly party games, at another the people may have had little in common, etc. This kind of comparison tends to bring out properties that an analogical comparison does not.

5. Simulate.   Simulation is the strategy of running a model of an object or event *x* to see what happens over a period of time under critical settings of different input variables (Stevens & Collins, 1980). It is the strategy that the chess master applies while trying to run out different possible alternative games, or that Young, Becker, and Pike (1970) advocate when they suggest viewing a concept as a dynamic process in order to generate ideas about the concept.

For example, one can simulate how the party or conversations during the party might have gone if different things had been said or different people had participated. Extrapolating further, one can consider how the party might have gone if everyone were in disguise, if the party were a Roman orgy, if the party were the last event before the end of the world, etc. Obviously the power of simulation derives from careful choice of critical cases in running the simulation.

6. Taxonomize.   The goal of the taxonomic strategy is to find a small set of invariants that provide an underlying explanation for the variation in the critical cases generated. This strategy is illustrated by Schank's (1972) taxonomy of primitive acts for representing different events in the world or Collins' (1977) taxonomy of the questioning strategies used by Socratic tutors.

For example, one might try to identify all the underlying factors that determine whether a party is interesting or boring. The list constructed might be: an optimal number of friends versus strangers, fast pace, no silly games, serving alcohol, etc. One tries to identify the entire set of characteristics that separate interesting parties from boring parties.

7. *Dimensionalize*.   A refinement on the taxonomic strategy is an attempt to find a small number of dimensions over which the critical cases vary in order to impose a structure on the set of taxonomic categories. An example of this strategy is fitting the chemical elements into the two dimensions of the periodic table.

To apply the dimensionalizing strategy to parties, one tries to identify the underlying dimensions on which the factors vary. For parties one might identify a dimension related to the nature and interrelations of the participants: how well they know each other, how much they have in common, how verbal or witty they are, etc. A second dimension might concern the activities at the party: whether they are fast paced or not, whether they are organized or freely chosen, whether they involve food and drink. Other dimensions might involve the length of time, the location, etc. The dimensionalizing strategy applies systematic analysis to determining the factors that affect a party's interestingness.

We can illustrate how these strategies are applied by describing the process of inventing ideas in two quite different domains: describing the taste of a banana, and creating a children's story about trucks and cars.

To describe the taste of a banana, the problem is to identify its taste with respect to the space of possible tastes. For example, in producing ideas about a banana's taste, one might:

1. Give the dependent variable, *taste,* so the first step is to generate as diverse a set of objects as possible ("critical cases") that cover the space of things whose taste is known (e.g., other fruits, vegetables, meats, candies, drinks, spices, etc.).

2. Compare a banana to each of these for differences. (Similarities are not crucial here.) It is not so tangy or juicy as an apricot, so crisp as an apple, so stringy as steak, so hot as pepper, etc. Notice that taste, smell, texture, etc. are all relevant here. At this stage, it is better to include anything that may be interesting, rather than restricting the question.

3. Simulate how the taste of a banana changes over time from when it is not ripe to when it is overripe. One can also simulate what a banana might taste like with other tastes such as ice cream or pepper.

4. Try to discover the underlying dimensions of the space of tastes. For example, one might come up with three main dimensions: flavor, texture, and aftertaste. Flavor might in turn break down into sweetness, tanginess, sourness, and saltiness, or some such taxonomy. Texture might break down into juiciness, crispness, and stringiness; aftertaste into strength, duration, and hotness.

5. Apply the comparison strategy recursively if one notices that the texture dimensions (at least crispness and stringiness) relate to the strength-of-materials literature. By analogy with materials, one can map onto the domain of foods

such dimensions as elasticity, ductility (brittleness), and strength, which form a new way of categorizing the texture of foods. Thus, one can compare the texture of foods to any knowledge one has about the strength of materials. In fact, one might go to a source book on materials to learn more about the different dimensions of their strength.

6. Run the analogy backward, from foods to materials, and ask why no correlate of juiciness apparently occurs in the literature on strength of materials. Juiciness will be seen to refer to the liquidity–solidity dimension: in-between states occur because liquids and solids are often intermixed in foods. The concern in the strength-of-materials literature is solely with solids that can be used as construction materials.

7. Finally, then, pinpoint where the taste of a banana lies in this three-dimensional space.

These same techniques can be applied to inventing ideas for fiction. We can illustrate this by sketching out their application to writing a children's story in the manner of Milne's (1926) *Winnie the Pooh*. In *Winnie the Pooh* Milne created the text by taking various toy animals that his son had, imbuing each with a human character based on certain salient characteristics of the animals, and creating incidents by simulating the kinds of interactions that come out of those characters.

To see this generation strategy in operation, the reader might try to apply it to creating a story about cars and trucks:

1. The first step is to generate critical cases—in this case, cars and trucks with as diverse characteristics as possible. For example, one might come up with a Volkswagen beetle, a fire truck, a Rolls-Royce, a cement mixer, etc.

2. By analogically mapping into the domain of human characters, we can create an identity (and even a name) for each vehicle. The Volkswagen might be a playful, cute little girl named Gretel. The fire truck might be a noisy, aggressive, bratty boy, always in a hurry, named Fred; the Rolls-Royce a haughty aristocrat named Algernon or Cecily; the cement mixer a tough hard-hat named Hank or Ida.

3. Given these characters, we can simulate the kinds of interactions they might have that generate the incidents around which story structures (Bruce, 1978; Mandler & Johnson, 1977; Rumelhart, 1975, 1977) must be imposed. For example, given a fire truck's habit of rushing past other vehicles while blowing its siren, and a Rolls-Royce's indisposition to be pushed aside by anyone, a chain of incidents and counter-incidents readily suggests itself.

These examples are designed to show how the manipulation strategies might be applied in producing a set of ideas for a text. The eventual goal of the theory is to describe these strategies more precisely.

TEXT PRODUCTION

The next stage is to impose text structures on the ideas. Text structures occur at different levels, with longer texts having more levels. For simplicity, we will assume that there are just four levels: the text level, the paragraph level, the sentence level (syntax), and the word level (spelling). In most of the discussion, we will be occupied with only the first three levels.

In this section we describe the different objectives that text structures are designed to achieve. Then we indicate how different devices can be used to accomplish these objectives. We also describe editing operators that can be applied to further these objectives. Finally we discuss how the process of imposing structure can be broken down into sequential steps, thus reducing the number of constraints that must be satisfied in any one step.

Different Objectives in Writing

We have identified four principles that form tacit objectives in writing. These objectives are realized by different structures and devices at different levels of the text. There are sometimes other objectives, such as producing dignified language or making a text legally unambiguous, but these four are the most pervasive goals of writing.

Making the Text Enticing.   To begin with, the writer must catch and hold the reader's attention. In conjunction with this, it is sometimes wisest to include the most interesting information in the beginning, in case the reader stops reading for some reason. There are a variety of devices designed to accomplish this objective: pyramid text form, the use of suspense or humor, using pictures, etc.

Making the Text Comprehensible.   The text should be as easy as possible for the reader to understand. The writer must give the reader enough clues to construct the correct model of the text. Some strategies that increase understandability are using examples to illustrate general principles, filling in intervening steps in arguments, and using short simple sentences.

Making the Text Rememberable.   The text should be structured so that the reader can hold its essential parts in memory. This quality goes beyond ease of understanding. A text can be easy to understand, but not very rememberable; magazine articles, for example, are often highly readable but nearly impossible to remember after a few days. In science the success of a theory often depends on the rememberability of its presentation; other scientists can only build on the theories they remember.

Rememberability is achieved in a number of ways at different levels of text. Using structures that are easy to recognize, such as tree structures, lists, and tables, is one important strategy. The use of hierarchical headings and of statements about the structure of the text also helps the reader organize the material to remember the key points. Experiments by Meyer (1975) and Thorndyke (1977) have shown how the structural aspects of a text affect people's ability to remember it.

Making the Text Persuasive.   In addition to understanding and remembering the ideas presented, the reader should also accept them. In expository text, this means that the reader should be convinced that the ideas are both important and true. In fiction, persuasiveness takes more forms; it can be directed to convincing the reader that the characters and plot development are natural and plausible, or that the themes embedded in the story are important insights about life. There are a number of devices used to make texts more persuasive: repetition of ideas, use of argument form, admission by the writer of any problems or limitations, calling forth experiences the reader is likely to have had, etc.

These tacit objectives of writing are realized by at least three different kinds of devices: what we have called structural devices, stylistic devices, and content devices. Unfortunately for the writer, there is no one-to-one correspondence between means and ends here. Sometimes a particular device serves several different objectives; alternatively, sometimes it may serve one objective, while interfering with other objectives. For example, as John Kenneth Galbraith (1978) has observed, the use of humor enhances enticingness but undercuts persuasiveness, because people don't take the ideas so seriously. Thus, it is important to consider different objectives in employing any particular device.

In different types of texts, each of these objectives may be more or less important. For example, in writing instructions for assembling a table, enticingness, rememberability, and persuasiveness are not important, whereas comprehensibility is important. On the other hand, in writing instructions for what to do in an airplane emergency, enticingness and rememberability become very important; airplane passengers must be enticed into reading the instructions and must remember them if an emergency occurs. Therefore, it is essential to determine how different devices affect each of these objectives so that the use of different devices can be optimized to serve the specific goals of a particular text.

Structural Devices

The objectives of writing can be achieved at different levels of text structure. We describe structural devices useful at the text, paragraph, and sentence levels, bearing in mind that in longer texts there are often additional intermediate levels.

We can illustrate the kinds of text-level forms that occur in writing with the following four examples:

Pyramid Form.   Any text can be structured so as to cover the most important ideas or events first and then to fill in more and more detail on succeeding passes through the material. Stories are covered this way in the newspaper so that readers can stop at different levels of detail. This is also an effective structure for texts designed to teach, because it covers material in the order easiest to learn (Collins, Warnock, & Passafiume, 1975; Norman, 1973).

Story or Narrative Form.   Any text can be structured according to the temporal and causal relations between the events that occurred. Story grammars (Mandler & Johnson, 1977; Rumelhart, 1975, 1977) attempt to give a formal characterization of story structure. Obviously most fiction uses some form of narrative structure, but it can be used in other forms of text as well. For example, scientists are using narrative structure when describing their thoughts and actions in a temporal sequence like a story unfolding (e.g., Miller, 1977). Devices such as suspense depend on using narrative structure.

Argument Form.   The Greeks developed several formulas for the structure of an oration. This kind of structure has passed down in part into the structure of such documents as legal briefs and scientific articles. One version of the form is: introduction, background, definition of issues, statement of what is to be proven, arguments for and against the thesis, refutation of opposing arguments, and summation (Lanham, 1969). Argument form is designed to be persuasive and is really only applicable to expository text.

Process-of-Elimination Form.   This is a kind of inverted pyramid structure where the writer makes an argument by eliminating all the possible alternatives (a form used by Bailyn, 1967). It is risky to use, because it often means taking up the least important and least interesting points first. We mention it because in writing it is important to consider what structures are good and what bad for achieving different objectives. Process-of-elimination structure can be good for persuading the reader, but it is usually bad for holding interest.

Paragraph structures are as diverse as text structures. A common paragraph structure consists of statement of thesis, elaboration of thesis, and summarization of thesis. In this scheme the elaboration can be realized in many different ways: by giving an example, by supplying supportive evidence, by filling out details. Other paragraph structures can be characterized as episodes within a narrative (Rumelhart, 1977) or as descriptions of scenes or objects (Meyer, 1975).

Sentence structures are usually the most diverse of all (though some writers use a small number of sentence frames quite successfully). One distinction among sentence types given by Strunk and White (1972) is that of a tight versus loose construction. For example,

1. Tight: "Because the store was closed, we went back home."
2. Loose: "The store was closed, and we went back home."

Sentence (1) is a tight construction, because it puts the given information in the first part of the sentence, the new information in the second part of the sentence (Haviland & Clark, 1974), and connects them in a strong way. This construction makes for ease of understanding and persuasiveness.

Sentence (2) is of the form "(Idea 1), and (Idea 2)," a loose construction that writers frequently overuse. In this construction there is no emphasis on the given–new distinction, nor does the conjunction specify how the two ideas are related. This lack of specificity is easy on the writer and hard on the reader.

Stylistic Devices

By stylistic devices, we refer to such elements in writing as metaphor, contrast, rhetorical questions, humor, suspense, etc. that are used by writers to create certain effects on readers. They are the means by which the writers satisfy many of the communicative-purpose constraints in writing. We include here the use of pictures, though they are unlike other stylistic devices. Like the structural devices, these stylistic devices exist at every level of text structure. We briefly discuss several of these devices and their implications for writing.

Metaphor. It is important to distinguish the use of metaphor as a strategy for inventing ideas (see earlier section) from its use as a stylistic device. As a stylistic device, it is a means of presenting an idea in terms of some other idea. It makes use of the basic notion that people readily understand new ideas in terms of their similarities with and differences from old ideas (Gentner, 1977a, 1977b; Moore & Newell, 1973). It can be used as a device within a sentence or throughout an entire text.

Because metaphor places a new topic in correspondence with well-learned old knowledge, it makes for ease of understanding and for high rememberability. However, it can also mislead the reader. This is because the mapping between the new idea and the old idea is never perfect. Unless the writer is very careful to make clear which properties of the old idea hold for the new idea and which do not, the reader may end up with a wrong, or partly wrong, conclusion. Another problem is that metaphors, like humor, call attention to themselves; in this case the reader may notice the glittering prose at the expense of the underlying ideas. These are arguments not for avoiding metaphor, but rather for using it thoughtfully.

Suspense. Suspense entails creating general expectations such that the reader cannot know precisely how they will be satisfied. Soap opera and mystery writers have a whole set of specific strategies for accomplishing this. Some of these strategies are specified by Schank and Abelson (1977) as expectation rules. One such strategy we extracted from a soap opera has the following form (which corresponds to Schank and Abelson's rule 3 on page 122): A character attributes an antagonistic action to another character. This creates an expectation that the first character will take some act of revenge against the other character.

Suspense, as a device, contributes chiefly to the enticingness of the writing. Often novice writers in science attempt to keep their readers in suspense in order to surprise them with their conclusion, beginning with an incorrect view and resolving with their true view of the topic. This use of suspense violates readers' expectations about the structure of scientific articles, because readers do not expect to see an incorrect view defended. If readers accept the incorrect view as that of the writer, the resulting confusion can be fairly serious. Thus, although suspense is enticing, it can interfere with comprehensibility and rememberability if used inappropriately.

Constructive Inference.   There is a device that some writers use to be persuasive that for lack of a better name we have called "constructive inference." The device involves providing enough clues to readers that they construct the idea the writer wants them to believe. Freud (1939) uses this device most effectively in *Moses and Monotheism* when he considers the possible reinterpretation of history if Moses were an Egyptian rather than a Jew. By providing clues about the relation between Ikhnaton's monotheism and Jewish monotheism, Freud encourages the reader to construct the idea that Moses was a disciple of Ikhnaton before he presents this idea as a conclusion. In this case and others Freud carefully musters evidence in an attempt to encourage the reader to draw Freud's own conclusion.

This device is used by magicians for persuasiveness. For example, rather than initially telling an audience that a deck of cards is a normal deck, a magician usually shows them the open deck, shuffles it, and in other ways treats it as normal. Magicians know that directly telling the audience something leads the audience to be suspicious, so they try to arrange things so that the audience makes the inference for itself. Constructive inference is a very powerful device for persuasion. Its potential dangers are that it can lack enticingness and comprehensibility.

Use of Pictures.   Pictures have several properties that affect the four writing objectives: (1) they tend to promote enticingness and so can help to hold onto the reader long enough to get information across; (2) they are often more rememberable than text (see Bower, 1972; Paivio, 1971); and (3) they can communicate spatial relations more easily than text, and therefore can increase the comprehensibility of text in this respect. However, pictures tend to be inferior to text in conveying certain abstract ideas, such as causality, and in conveying temporal sequences.

Content Devices

Content devices are those that spring fairly directly from the nature of the ideas being discussed. Generally, use of one content device or another requires that the writer carefully consider the nature of the message that is to be conveyed.

There are three elements of the underlying idea structure that have strong effects on the comprehensibility and rememberability of texts. We refer to these as the hierarchical structuring of the ideas, the tangibility of the ideas, and the connectivity of the ideas.

Hierarchical Structure.   The surface form of a text is a linear structure, but underlying the linear structure is a higher-level organization of ideas (Brown, Collins, & Harris, 1978; Meyer, 1975). Although this underlying structure can be hierarchical to a greater or lesser degree, there is probably some optimum balance to achieve clarity and rememberability. Too flat a structure overloads one's ability to remember all the parallel elements; too deep a structure overloads one's ability to remember all the levels of embedding and to keep straight the interrelationships. Probably, a branching hierarchical structure with three to six elements at each branch is optimal (Mandler, 1967).

Tangibility.   Tangibility involves the feeling of coherence, unity, and identifiability of an idea. Ideas at all levels can be more or less tangible. Probably the simplest way to make an idea tangible is to name it. For example, we are using this device here, by assigning the name *tangibility* to this notion of perceived unity and coherence. When an idea is named, it takes on some of the conceptual properties of a simple object (Gentner, 1978a, 1978b). It acquires a feeling of simplicity and unity that makes it more accessible in memory and easier to attach other relationships or properties to. We are able to take a complex network of relations and give this entire network a noun name, and, having done this, to then treat this entire complex structure as though it were a single node. This is one of the great capabilities of civilized man. It is the way in which abstract terms allow us to bootstrap our way into conceptual structures that go well beyond our perceptual limitations.

This kind of hierarchical collapsing has both great power and also certain dangers. The power is that it allows us to talk about causes and effects and interrelations between huge bodies of conceptual data, which can make the text more rememberable. But at the same time, overuse of this device can make a text sound full of jargon and thus less comprehensible and persuasive.

Connectivity.   An important aspect of writing is maintaining connective flow. The relationships between ideas must be made clear. In order to write about an idea, its description must be expanded downward in terms of the successively lower levels of paragraphs, sentences, words, and letters. This requires a great many processes, most of which are irrelevant to the high-level connections among ideas. Having produced an expansion of the first idea, the writer must jump back up to the idea level to recall the desired connection. Then there must be a similarly detailed expansion of the second idea, together with an indication of the relationship between the two ideas. Making clear the connections between ideas is important for comprehensibility, rememberability, and persuasiveness.

Editing

Most writers feel that editing is as crucial an aspect of good writing as is initial text production. Thus, when one teaches writing, a major goal should be to teach writers to step back and look at their text from another person's point of view (Scardamalia, Bereiter, & McDonald, 1977). As a prescriptive method to teach editing, it is useful to teach students the editing operators that skilled writers acquire after extensive practice at writing.

Editing operators, which exist at each level of text structure, for the most part parallel the structural and content devices discussed earlier. They also reflect the kinds of errors writers typically make. We list some of the editing operators that writers should learn to apply. None of these operators, of course, can be blindly applied in any situation.

Some text-level operators are:

1. *Delete extraneous material.* Generally, any sections of text that nothing else depends on should be deleted.
2. *Add headings and plan of text.* Anything done to make structure of text more visible helps the reader to understand and remember the text.
3. *Move important ideas to front.* If the most interesting or important ideas are buried in the middle of the text, the reader may never find them.
4. *Qualify at beginning, not in each sentence.* If there is a need to qualify a whole section of text, move all the qualifications into a general statement at the beginning.

Some paragraph level operators are:

1. *Shorten long paragraphs.* Long paragraphs are hard to read and hard to remember, so the writer should shorten them where possible.
2. *Make lists or tables.* When discussing a whole series of ideas, it helps comprehension to put these into lists or tables in which the conceptual structure can be spatially clarified.
3. *Add topic and concluding sentences.* In exposition, paragraphs should start with a topic sentence and conclude with a summary sentence.
4. *Put in connective phrases.* Phrases like "therefore" and "nevertheless" can make clear the relation between different ideas in the paragraph.

Some sentence-level operators are:

1. *Delete empty words and phrases.* There are a number of rather mechanical words and phrases that can often be deleted from text, such as ''seems to be,'' ''possibly,'' ''as a matter of fact,'' etc.
2. *Create parallel structures.* Sentences are difficult to understand if parallel structure isn't maintained in different clauses or phrases.
3. *Break long sentences into shorter sentences.* If a sentence is too long, it helps comprehensibility to make two sentences out of the one. A rule practiced by some writers is ''One idea per sentence.''
4. *Turn passive sentences into active sentences.* Passive sentences often entail awkward constructions, which can be eliminated by a change to active voice.

These give some of the more common editing operators experienced writers use. Specifying these operators could be of enormous benefit for teaching writing.

The Process of Producing Text

Separating the various steps in producing text helps the writer in two ways: It simultaneously eases the number of constraints that must be satisfied at one time and it increases the likelihood of satisfying any particular constraint.

One useful step-by-step procedure is as follows:

1. Create a detailed outline of the text structure.
2. Apply text-level editing operators.
3. Create a semitext with all the ideas included in paragraphs, but not in finished sentences.
4. Apply paragraph-level editing operators.
5. Create finished sentence-level text.
6. Apply sentence-level editing operators.

This step-by-step approach helps the writer because much of the necessary editing can be done before producing finished text. It also allows the writer to concentrate on generation and editing with respect to one aspect of the text at a time. But it is important that the writer think of the outline on semitext as modifiable; too often outlines are treated as rigid entities. The disadvantage of this step-by-step approach is that it is slower to produce text this way. But where writer's block is a problem, this process can help to overcome it.

WHAT MAKES WRITING DIFFICULT TO LEARN

Much of the difficulty of writing stems from the large number of constraints that must be satisfied at the same time. In expressing an idea the writer must consider at least four structural levels: overall text structure, paragraph structure, sentence structure (syntax), and word structure (spelling). Clearly the attempt to coordinate all these requirements is a staggering job. What makes the learning process particularly difficult, however, is that the whole set of task components must be learned at once. The child has no opportunity to set aside the problems of spelling and syntax while learning to produce paragraph structures. Teaching methods should be designed to allow the beginning writer to practice fewer task components at a time in a meaningful way.

One great difficulty for writers is maintaining *connective flow*. The relationships between ideas must be made clear. Yet in order to write about an idea, the idea must be expanded downward into paragraphs, sentences, words, and letters. Sometimes writers—particularly children—become lost in the process of downward expansion and lose sight of the high-level relationships they originally wanted to express. *Downsliding*—the phenomenon of getting pulled into lower and more local levels of task processing—is a very common problem in writing, and in other domains as well. If a teacher emphasizes accuracy in spelling and grammar, it will reinforce the natural tendency toward downsliding. The overall result will be that children focus almost exclusively on lower-level task components when they write.

Scardamalia's (in press) observations of children's prose illustrate their difficulties in maintaining connective flow. She gives many examples in which idea-level relationships are inadequately expressed, even though the lower-level structures of syntax and spelling are quite good. The developmental increase in the number of ideas that can be coordinated probably reflects the fact that older children are more practiced at text production. This means that the lower levels of structure no longer occupy all their attention, allowing them to spend more resources coordinating ideas.

A COMPUTER-BASED "WRITING LAND"

Our society is now in the midst of a revolution in the way texts are produced and edited. More and more sophisticated computer text-editors are coming into use that allow writers to do things easily that are quite difficult to do with pen and paper. They also are rapidly becoming less expensive.

We think there are several ways that this technology can be exploited for teaching and assisting people in writing. In particular, we think a computer-based text system might contain a set of activities designed to teach different aspects of the writing process described previously. It might also be possible to create a writing assistant that gives advice on writing as the person carries out some writing task. Such a computer-based text system could be called "Writing Land."

Current Developments in Text Editors

Text-editing systems for producing documents, either on small stand-alone computers or on large computers, are now becoming commonplace. Text is produced by typing it into the computer's memory, from which a paper copy can be produced at any time. There is a set of commands that enables a person to move a piece of text from one part of a document to another, replace any piece of text, and insert new text anywhere. Because such a system makes editing much easier, documents typically go through many more drafts than without such a system.

Another capability that many text-editing systems have is to detect spelling errors for the user. When a document is complete, the user can run a spelling corrector that prints out all the words it does not recognize (including most proper nouns).

A system that has recently been developed by Teitelman (1977) allows the user to move pages of text on a screen as if they were on a desk top. Thus, the user can type his ideas onto different pages like note cards and assemble a text from the separate pages.

Embedding Tasks in Writing Land

We have shown how it is possible to break down the writing process into component subprocesses. In order to teach writing, the teacher can give the student tasks that exercise these subprocesses individually. These intermediate tasks can be embedded in a "Writing Land" text system.

We can illustrate the kinds of intermediate writing tasks we envision:

1. Given a set of ideas about some topic (which are stored in Writing Land), the first task for students might be to group them. We can evaluate different aspects of their grouping strategies, such as how much hierarchical structure they impose and whether they throw out irrelevant ideas.

2. A second task might be to create three outlines for the set of ideas: one in pyramid form, one in argument form, and one in narrative form. This teaches students how the same set of ideas can be organized in different high-level text structures.

3. A third task might be to assemble the ideas into text, following one of the outlines.

We could also give students a variety of editing tasks:

1. Students could be given a badly written text and asked to apply the various editing operators listed previously. They could be evaluated in terms of which kinds of editing operators they apply and which edits they miss.
2. Students could be given a badly structured outline in argument form and asked to revise it.

If the set of ideas or text that the student is to work with is constrained, it may be possible for the computer to evaluate at least some aspects of the student's performance automatically. Thus it could be a powerful tool for assisting teachers of writing.

A Writing Assistant

A cognitive theory of writing can suggest ways in which the Writing Land program can assist the writer during work on various writing tasks. The system might advise the writer about the following kinds of information:

1. What strategies are appropriate to apply in each stage for the kind of text being written.
2. What text structures are appropriate for the type of text being written.
3. What editing operators should be applied in each stage.

The spelling-correction scheme might be extended to look for other possible types of editing changes; for example, to suggest sentences or paragraphs that might be shortened, to check for overuse of "and" to connect independent clauses (Strunk & White, 1972), or even to identify some kinds of sentences that are not well formed (Woods, 1970). Thus the systems have a potential to make editorial suggestions to users.

A Reading and Writing Environment

Another possibility inherent in Writing Land is to create a reading and writing environment with highly motivating, meaningful activities for students. We mention two representative activities that are currently available using large computers.

1. There are now electronic mail facilities associated with several computer networks. These facilities allow a person to type a message to another person who has access to the network. The message is transmitted instantaneously, and as soon as the receiver logs onto the computer, notice is given that a message is

waiting. A few commands can then be typed to retrieve the message. Rubinstein and Goldenberg (1978) encouraged deaf children to use electronic mail to send messages to each other and to the teacher (like passing notes). Many of the children used the system. For several of the children, the quality of the messages improved dramatically over time.

2. A computer game that many children and adults find captivating is called Adventure. In it, the player tries to explore underground caves in order to find buried treasure, while fighting off dragons and malevolent little elves. Players type commands in simple English in order to move from place to place or to pick up things. After each command, they receive a message that tells the result of the action. With more sophisticated language-understanding capabilities, this kind of reading and writing game could be made into a highly motivating educational activity.

CONCLUSION

In this chapter we have tried to indicate what we think are the major elements needed to construct a theory of writing. This formulation is only a beginning. There is much to be done in organizing these elements into a predictive theory. We believe that the factors we have discussed here will be useful in the eventual theoretical formulation and also that this work can have practical implications for the teaching and practice of writing.

One may wonder where in all these rather specific processes and suggested strategies lies scope for the truly creative student who has potential to be a brilliant writer. It is our feeling that such a student can only benefit from having the heuristics for composition stated as clearly and as well as it is possible to state them. A brilliant student will eventually go beyond the rules, either by creating additional relationships or else by breaking with the forms altogether. But, just as Beethoven benefited from his lessons in composition from Haydn, so even the most creative student can benefit from clear knowledge of the present state of the art.

ACKNOWLEDGMENTS

This research was supported by the National Institute of Education under Contract No. MS-NIE-C-400-76-0116. We thank Chip Bruce, Andee Rubin, Linda Flower, and John Seeley Brown for their contributions to our thinking on these issues, and Radia Perlman and Erwin R. Steinberg for their comments on a previous draft of the chapter. We especially thank Jill O'Brien for enduring a hundred drafts of the chapter.

REFERENCES

Bailyn, B. *The ideological origin of the American revolution.* Cambridge, Mass.: Harvard University Press, 1967.

Bartlett, F. C. *Remembering.* Cambridge, Mass.: The University Press, 1932.

Bower, G. H. Mental imagery and associative learning. In L. W. Gregg (Ed.), *Cognition in learning and memory.* New York: Wiley, 1972.

Brown, J. S., Collins, A., & Harris, G. Artificial intelligence and learning strategies. In H. F. O'Neill (Ed.), *Learning strategies.* New York: Academic Press, 1978.

Bruce, B. C. Interacting plans. *Cognitive Science,* 1978, *2,* 195–233.

Chomsky, N. *Syntactic structures.* The Hague: Mouton, 1957.

Collins, A. Processes in acquiring knowledge. In R. C. Anderson, R. J. Spiro, & W. E. Montague (Eds.), *Schooling and the acquisition of knowledge.* Hillsdale, N.J.: Lawrence Erlbaum Associates, 1977.

Collins, A., Warnock, E. H., Aiello, N., & Miller, M. L. Reasoning from incomplete knowledge. In D. Bobrow & A. Collins (Eds.), *Representation and understanding: Studies in cognitive science.* New York: Academic Press, 1975.

Collins, A., Warnock, E. H., & Passafiume, J. J. Analysis and synthesis of tutorial dialogs. In G. H. Bower (Ed.), *The psychology of learning and motivation* (Vol. 9). New York: Academic Press, 1975.

Flower, L. S., & Hayes, J. R. Problem solving and the cognitive process of writing. In C. H. Frederiksen, M. F. Whiteman, & J. F. Dominic (Eds.), *Writing: The nature, development and teaching of written communication.* Hillsdale, N.J.: Lawrence Erlbaum Associates, in press.

Freud, S. *Moses and monotheism.* New York: A. A. Knopf, 1939.

Galbraith, J. K. Writing, typing & economics. *The Atlantic Monthly,* March 1978, *241* (3), 102–105.

Gentner, D. G. Children's performance on a spatial analogies task. *Child Development,* 1977, *48,* 1034–1039. (a)

Gentner, D. G. If a tree had a knee, where would it be? Children's performance on simple spatial metaphors. *Papers and Reports on Child Language Development,* 1977, *13.* (b)

Gentner, D. On relational meaning: The acquisition of verb meaning. *Child Development,* 1978, *49*(4), 988–998. (a)

Gentner, D. *Semantic integration of word meanings.* (Report No. 3826). Cambridge, Mass.: Bolt Beranek and Newman Inc., May 1978. (b)

Gleason, H. A. *An introduction to descriptive linguistics.* (Rev. ed.). New York: Holt, Rinehart & Winston, 1961.

Hall, D. *Writing well.* Boston, Mass.: Little, Brown & Co., 1973.

Haviland, S. E., & Clark, H. H. What's new? Acquiring new information as a process in comprehension. *Journal of Verbal Learning and Verbal Behavior,* 1974, *13,* 512–521.

Lanham, R. A. *A handlist of rhetorical terms.* Berkeley, Calif.: University of California Press, 1969.

Mandler, G. Organization and memory. In K. W. Spence & J. A. Spence (Eds.), *The psychology of learning and motivation* (Vol. 1). New York: Academic Press, 1967.

Mandler, J. M., & Johnson, N. S. Remembrance of things parsed: Story structure and recall. *Cognitive Psychology,* 1977, *9,* 111–151.

Meyer, B. J. F. *The organization of prose and its effects on memory.* Amsterdam: North-Holland Publishing Company, 1975.

Miller, G. A. *Spontaneous apprentices: Children and language.* New York: Seabury Press, 1977.

Milne, A. A. *Winnie the pooh.* New York: E. P. Dutton, 1926.

Moore, J., & Newell, A. How can MERLIN understand? In L. Gregg (Ed.), *Knowledge and cognition*. Hillsdale, N.J.: Lawrence Erlbaum Associates, 1973.

Norman, D. A. Memory, knowledge, and the answering of questions. In R. L. Solso (Ed.), *Contemporary issues in cognitive psychology: The Loyola Symposium*. New York: Halsted Press, 1973.

Paivio, A. *Imagery and verbal processes*. New York: Holt, Rinehart & Winston, 1971.

Rubinstein, R., & Goldenberg, P. Using a computer message system for promoting reading and writing in a school for the deaf. *Proceedings of the Fifth Annual Conference on Systems for the Disabled*. Houston, June, 1978.

Rumelhart, D. E. Notes on a schema for stories. In D. Bobrow & A. Collins (Eds.), *Representation and understanding: Studies in Cognitive Science*. New York: Academic Press, 1975.

Rumelhart, D. E. Understanding and summarizing brief stories. In D. LaBerge & J. Samuels (Eds.), *Basic processes in reading: Perception and comprehension*. Hillsdale, N.J.: Lawrence Erlbaum Associates, 1977.

Scardamalia, M. How children cope with the cognitive demands of writing. In C. H. Frederiksen, M. F. Whiteman, & J. F. Dominic (Eds.), *Writing: The nature, development and teaching of written communication*. Hillsdale, N.J.: Lawrence Erlbaum Associates, in press.

Scardamalia, M., Bereiter, C., & McDonald, J. D. S. *Role taking in written communication investigated by manipulating anticipatory knowledge*. Paper presented at the biennial meeting of the Society for Research in Child Development, New Orleans, March 1977. (ERIC Document Reproduction Service No. ED 151 792)

Schank, R. Conceptual dependency: A theory of natural language understanding. *Cognitive Psychology*, 1972, *3*, 552–631.

Schank, R., & Abelson, R. *Scripts, plans, goals, and understandings*. Hillsdale, N.J.: Lawrence Erlbaum Associates, 1977.

Stevens, A. L., & Collins, A. Multiple conceptual models of a complex system. In R. Snow, P. Federico, & W. Montague (Eds.), *Aptitude, learning and instruction: Cognitive process analysis*. Hillsdale, N.J.: Lawrence Erlbaum Associates, 1980.

Strunk, W., & White, E. B. *The elements of style*. New York: Macmillan, 1972.

Teitelman, W. A display oriented programmer's assistant. *Proceedings of the Fifth International Joint Conference on Artificial Intelligence*, 1977, 905–915.

Thorndyke, P. W. Cognitive structures in comprehension and memory of narrative discourse. *Cognitive Psychology*, 1977, *9*, 77–110.

Wason, P. The context of plausible denial. *Journal of Verbal Learning and Verbal Behavior*, 1965, *4*, 7–11.

Winston, P. H. *Artificial intelligence*. Reading, Mass.: Addison-Wesley, 1977.

Woods, W. A. Transition network grammars for natural language analysis. *Communications of the ACM*, 1970, *13*, 591–606.

Young, R. E., Becker, A. L., & Pike, K. L. *Rhetoric: Discovery and change*. New York: Harcourt, Brace, & World, 1970.

4 Development in Writing

Carl Bereiter
Ontario Institute for Studies in Education

Although there is a substantial body of data on the development of writing skills, it has not seemed to have much implication for instruction. Reviews of writing research from an educational perspective have given scant attention to it (Blount, 1973; Braddock, Lloyd-Jones, & Schoer, 1963; Lyman, 1929; West, 1967). Generally speaking, developmental research has educational significance only when there is a conceptual apparatus linking it with questions of practical significance.

Almost all of the data on writing development consist of frequency counts—words per communication unit, incidence of different kinds of dependent clauses, frequency of different types of writing at different ages, and so on. The conceptual frameworks used for interpreting these data have come largely from linguistics (e.g., Hunt, 1963; Loban, 1976; O'Donnell, Griffin, & Norris, 1967). However informative these analyses might be to the student of language development, they are disappointing from an educational point of view. The variables they look at seem unrelated to commonly held purposes of writing instruction (Nystrand, 1977).

The purpose of this chapter is to synthesize findings on the growth of writing skills within what may be called an "applied cognitive-developmental" framework. Key issues within such a framework are the cognitive strategies children use and how these are adapted to their limited information-processing capacities (Case, 1975, 1978; Klahr & Wallace, 1976; Scardamalia, in press). Although this chapter does not deal with instructional implications, it becomes evident that the issues considered within an applied cognitive-developmental framework are relevant to such concerns of writing instruction as fluency, coherence, correctness, sense of audience, style, and thought content.

WHAT IS DEVELOPMENT IN WRITING?

Students' writing will undoubtedly reflect their overall language development (Loban, 1976; O'Donnell et al., 1967) and also their level of cognitive development (Collis & Biggs, undated; Scardamalia, in press). It is to be expected that it will also at times reflect their level of moral development, social cognition, etc. Given the small role that writing plays in most children's lives, it is therefore reasonable to suppose that there is no such thing as writing development as such—that it is merely the resultant of other, more basic kinds of development. This view is implicit in the speech-primacy position of researchers like Loban (1963, 1966, 1976), who treat children's writing simply as another source of data on their language development.

However, although it may be reasonable to treat writing development as a reflection of other kinds of development, it is not very useful to do so. An educationally relevant account of writing development would have to give prominence to whatever is distinctive about writing and potentially susceptible to direct influence. The following have been recognized as distinctive characteristics of writing:

1. Written English may be recognized as a subsystem of English, along with spoken English, and distinguishable from the latter in a number of ways. It is usually more compact, contains more elaborately specified subjects, shows less local variation than spoken English, and shows a different distribution of linguistic devices and usages (Allen, 1972; Gleason, 1965; Long, 1961).

2. Written English and spoken English are predominately, but not exclusively, tied to different modalities. One may speak written English, as in dictation, or write spoken English, as in composing dialogue. Unpublished data collected by P. J. Gamlin show that children as young as age eight can differentiate sharply between writing spoken English and writing written English, although there is a tendency for them to drift into writing spoken English. Use of the two subsystems is evidently quite situation-sensitive. Moscovici and Plon (1966) found that when people are seated back-to-back, their conversational speech takes on the characteristics of written language, whereas it has the characteristics of spoken language when they are seated face-to-face, even when there is a screen between them.

3. Written English involves a number of conventions not pertinent to spoken English—spelling, punctuation, paragraph indentation, etc. What is especially noteworthy about these conventions, as compared to the conventions of spoken language, is that they are learned almost exclusively in school (Allen, 1972).

4. Writing may require and thus foster a different kind of thought from that involved in speaking (Goody & Watt, 1963; Havelock, 1973; Olson, 1977). Because writers get little feedback and because they must address unknown readers in unknown contexts who have unknown states of knowledge, writers

are forced to develop what Olson (1977) calls "essayist technique"—a form of discourse characterized by explicit reference and by propositions linked together by logical entailment rather than by reference to experience shared between writer and reader.

5. Finally, because written utterances can be more deliberately shaped and reshaped than spoken ones, writing lends itself to the development of craftsman-like skills not normally found in speaking. For the same reason writing also lends itself to complex productions that would be very difficult to achieve in the oral mode—for instance, novels, sonnets, and scholarly works.

The preceding observations suggest that a useful account of development in writing should deal with: (1) the gradual differentiation of written from spoken language, as distinct subsystems; (2) development of ability to switch appropriately between the systems; (3) mastery of the conventions peculiar to written language; (4) development of explicit, objective, context-free propositional language; and (5) achievement of literary style and proficiency in various genres of written composition.

Studies comparing spoken and written language development have indeed shown a gradual differentiation of the two. In the early school years the mean T-unit length[1] of spoken utterances is greater than that of written ones and somewhere in the middle school years this difference reverses, in keeping with the tendency of mature written language to be more elaborated than spoken language (Loban, 1976; O'Donnell et al., 1967).

Data more directly indicative of mastery of writing skills have not shown such regular growth, however. Global ratings of quality of written compositions in the National Assessment of Educational Progress (1975) show that substantial gains in quality occur between the ages of 9 and 13, but little or no gain occurs between the ages of 13 and 17.[2] Hill (1972), on the other hand, found no natural growth or development in the use of specifically literary devices of genre or form; all devices could be found in children's writing, but with a low incidence at all ages.

Although Loban (1976), in his 12-year longitudinal study of written and oral language development, found steady trends in gross indicators of quantity and complexity of verbal output, trends in the use of specific language devices tended to be more wobbly. For instance, whereas the use of dependent clauses in oral language increased steadily from year to year and always distinguished high ability from low ability students, the same was not true in written language. For students of high and average ability, use of dependent clauses leveled off after

---

[1]A T-unit is the minimal unit that can be punctuated as a sentence (whether the writer has punctuated it that way or not).

[2]In both the 1969 and the 1974 NAEP testings, 17-year-olds scored slightly higher than 13-year-olds. If we compare the 17-year-olds of 1974 with the 13-year-olds of 1969, however, we find no gain, and these two groups represent approximately the same age cohort.

grade 8, and low ability students overtook them by grade 10. Loban's interpretation was that by that time the more able students were finding alternative means of embedding. In general it seems that frequency-count indicators of growth become equivocal when applied to specific usages, because linguistic devices are often substitutable one for another, so that increase in the use of one may result in decrease in the use of another. Quality indicators may also show unstable trends because of regressions due to the introduction of new skills into the writer's repertoire. Diebel and Sears (1917) put it well decades ago when they noted that some errors in writing increase with age because "as the child's mind grows he will use more complicated forms of expression [p. 175]."

These ambiguities in frequency-count findings suggest that lying behind the quantitative trends in writing development may be more interesting qualitative changes, changes in the *way* children go about writing. Research aimed at discovering such qualitative changes has been rare, however.

Loban (1976) stated that one of the purposes of his longitudinal study was to investigate the question, "Can definite stages of language development be identified? [p. 2]." In the end he was able to provide qualitatively distinct descriptions of the language of children at different ages, but what they nevertheless generally add up to is the gradual acquisition of mature characteristics. As Loban (1976) observed, his data "very often show a steady nondramatic chronological development. This would indicate that linguistic 'stages' are no more discrete, no more sudden, than the stages of physical growth reported by Gesell and Ilg [pp. 84–85]." In none of his "stage" descriptions does Loban note anything special about writing development. He does, however, observe that there is a plateau in oral language development running from grade 7 to grade 9 or 10 and that this plateau comes a year later in written language.

The most ambitious attempt to identify qualitative changes in writing abilities is the Schools Council study of English students of ages 11 to 18 (Britton, Burgess, Martin, McLeod, & Rosen, 1975). This research was based on samples of writing done in all curriculum areas. Compositions were classified according to a complex model of written language functions and writer–reader relationships. Without explicating the model, which is impossible in this review, the findings cannot be adequately conveyed. One major finding, however, stands out above all the complexities. It is the overriding influence of school demands on student writing. Although there was some evidence of a developmental trend toward writing for a larger audience, it was overshadowed by a trend (presumably school-induced) toward writing to the teacher as examiner. The authors hypothesized a branching developmental trend from relatively undisciplined "expressive" writing to "transactional" and "poetic" writing. Data generally supported the hypothesis, except that there was a drastic decline in the frequency of "poetic" writing in the oldest age group. This shift was attributed, not to natural tendencies, but to the influence of the examination system. Thus, the disappointing message of the Schools Council research is that as soon as we begin to look beyond syntax, vocabulary, and the like and try to investigate functional aspects of student writing, we begin to find out more about the school system than we find out about children.

A research approach that shows promise of getting at qualitative changes in writing competence has been reported by Stahl (1974, 1977), who has devised an instrument for describing structural characteristics of compositions on a particular topic—"My Home." Applying this instrument to compositions written by Israeli children in grades 2, 5, and 8, Stahl (1977) obtained results that could be interpreted as showing a stage shift between grades 2 and 8 (although Stahl interpreted them as showing gradual improvement). The modal compositions in grades 2 and 8 were alike in showing no evidence of planning or structural revision and no indicated order of presentation. However, the modal grade 8 composition followed a general principle for selecting content, presented the content in a coherent ("guided tour") arrangement, and allocated space in proportion to the importance of elements, whereas the modal grade 2 composition showed no evidence of attention to selection, arrangement, or balance. The typical grade 8 composition ended at an appropriate point, whereas the typical grade 2 composition just broke off. It is the grade 5 compositions, however, that provide support for a stage shift interpretation of these differences. Instead of falling into intermediate categories between those occupied by the grade 2 and grade 8 compositions, they tended to be bimodally distributed, some showing the grade 8 characteristics and others showing the grade 2 characteristics.

What is encouraging about Stahl's approach is that it begins to tell us something about the writer instead of about the writer's product. It begins to suggest a different and more elaborate system of skills operating in grade 8 students from that operating in grade 2 students. Nonetheless Stahl's, along with all the other developmental research cited, is what Nystrand (1977) calls "text-based" as opposed to "writer-based." It looks for what is achieved in the written product rather than using the written product to infer what is inside the writer—that is, what constitutes the writer's compentence or executive system.

However, although "Look at the process, not the product" is a fine precept, writing researchers of the past should not be criticized for their failure to follow it. Following this precept, and thus advancing toward an understanding of how the process of writing develops in children, requires a psychological model of the writing process; and work on developing cognitive process models of writing has only recently begun.

WRITING AS A
COGNITIVE PROCESS

Although no complete cognitive processing model of writing has yet been advanced, several beginnings have been made. Hayes and Flower (Chapter 1) have been extracting, from protocols of writers "thinking aloud," the basic moves or strategic elements that writers use in written composition. Nold (in press) has attempted to sort out different levels of processing that go on in revising, levels that clearly have their counterparts in composition. Scardamalia (in press) has looked specifically at how immature writers adapt writing tasks to fit within their limited information-processing capacities. A complete processing model would have to deal with all three of these aspects—with the cognitive moves that make up writing and their organization; with levels of processing, from the highly conscious and intentional to the unconscious and automatic; and with how processing capacity is deployed to these various functions in such a way as to enable writing to go on.

Because an understanding of the development of writing abilities depends on such a model, it is worth considering what a complete model of the writing process might be like, even if it can be sketched only roughly. A sketch is possible even at this early stage of cognitive research into writing because a model of written composition will necessarily have much in common with models of speech production (e.g., Fodor, Bever, & Garrett, 1974) and of language comprehension (e.g., Adams & Collins, 1977).

There will be a high-level executive scheme directing the whole writing operation in keeping with certain purposes and constraints. At the next lower level will be what in writing we may wish to call "genre" schemes. A genre scheme consists, essentially, of the knowledge available for directing a certain kind of writing. The person who has never before written a mystery story is likely nevertheless to have available a mystery story scheme that will direct the novice writer to think of a crime, a crime-solver, a way of bringing the solver into contact with the crime, a puzzling element, etc., that will call for keeping the identity of the criminal secret till the end, and that may call for certain stereotyped events, characters, and expressions. The experienced mystery writer will have a more elaborate genre scheme that will set more sophisticated requirements and direct more complex searches and constructions.

In order to consider the functions of a genre scheme, let us take a more everyday example, that of a "letter of recommendation" scheme. The teacher or supervisor experienced in writing such letters will have a scheme that includes the following:

1. A limited set of fairly specific *intentions:* e.g., to present the candidate in the best possible light, to do the candidate no harm but to avoid explicit commitment, etc.

2. A set of *strategies* or *game plans* appropriate to carrying out these intentions. A game plan will in turn include the following.

3. *Categories of content* needed to support the plan. These may be in the nature of slots to be filled: "The candidate has shown initiative by _____ and _____."

4. *Search procedures* for discovering the needed content. These may be overt procedures such as consulting certain records or calling on informants, or they may be internal memory-search strategies.

5. *Tuning instructions* for language output. For instance, a typical game plan might call for expressing the recommendation in language that is standard written English, fairly formal, dense, authoritative, and vague. But another strategy might call for quite different language.

The beginner, who has never before written a letter of recommendation and who may not even have read one, will lack a specific scheme for this genre and will have to use some other available scheme—such as a general business letter scheme or a scholarly writing scheme. These schemes will also contain intentions, game plans, categories of content, search procedures, and tuning instructions, but they will be less finely adapted to the task of writing a letter of recommendation. That means that a great deal more feedback and revision of higher-level decisions in the light of lower-level outputs will be required. If the beginner is a generally skillful writer, the result may well be an adequate letter of recommendation, but it may take the beginner 10 times as long to achieve the same result as it takes the writer who has a well-developed scheme for that genre.

Below the genre scheme will be a *content processor* that draws semantic material from memory and organizes it according to instructions from the genre scheme. Its output is what we may call a *gist*—a unit of content not yet formed into overt language. The *gist* then goes to a *language processor* that puts it into explicit language, according to tuning instructions from the genre scheme. The content and language processors, we may assume, are of an all-purpose sort and are not specialized for genres nor even to writing as opposed to speaking. What they do that is unique to writing depends on instructions from writing genre schemes.

This simple step-at-a-time process is sure to be enormously complicated by continual comparisons between instructions and outputs, with resulting changes in processing or in higher-level decisions or in both. Without going into detail, we may simply note the extreme case, which is likely to be familiar to any experienced writer—the case where difficulty in finding the right word starts a chain of adjustments at successively higher levels until finally the intention of the whole composition is altered.

By the time children have acquired the basic mechanics of writing, they probably have available the whole hierarchy of processing levels that adults have, even though the schemes or mechanisms at each level may be undeveloped and little differentiated. It is clear that young children can formulate intentions (Hunt, 1963), broadly differentiate their writing according to genres such as narrative, dialogue, exposition, and verse (Hill, 1972), and tune their language output to suit different audiences (Shatz & Gelman, 1973).

One interpretation of writing development might therefore be that it consists of the gradual elaboration and refinement of relevant schemes at different processing levels. This is the view that seems to be implicit in most school approaches to writing instruction, where pupils at all grade levels do pretty much the same thing—write stories, essays, etc.—and the teacher tries to help students along with all aspects of writing at once. Such a view is undoubtedly correct in that learning inevitably takes place at all levels at once. For an analysis of writing development to stop there, however, is for it to overlook all that is most difficult about learning to write.

INFORMATION-PROCESSING LOAD IN WRITING

The preceding sketch of a process model of writing only weakly suggests the number of things that must be dealt with more-or-less simultaneously in writing. As Scardamalia (in press) observes:

> Even a casual analysis makes it clear that the number of things that must be dealt with simultaneously in writing is stupendous: handwriting, spelling, punctuation, word choice, syntax, textual connections, purpose, organization, clarity, rhythm, euphony, the possible reactions of various possible readers, and so on. To pay conscious attention to all of these would overload the information-processing capacity of the most towering intellects.

Although some of these matters could be dealt with sequentially instead of simultaneously, it appears that most writers do not do so. Emig (1971), questioning mature and practicing writers, found few who planned before writing, developed text from outline, etc. Stallard (1974), examining the writing behavior of "good" as well as randomly selected student writers, again found that both kinds tended simply to plunge into the task and try to do everything at once. Our own informal observations of careful writers suggest that they do most of their revising as they go along, instead of treating revision as a separate segment of the writing process.

In order for writers to carry on such a variety of processes simultaneously, either or more likely both of the following conditions must obtain: (1) automatization of many parts of the writing process so that they can be carried on with infrequent or slight conscious attention (Posner & Keele, 1973); and (2) highly skilled time-sharing, so that attention can range over a number of ongoing tasks without serious lapses or interference. Such performance would also seem to require attainment of adult levels of working memory capacity—if indeed this capacity grows with age (Pascual-Leone, 1970; Simon, 1972, 1974).

The only known attempt at a quantitative analysis of information-processing load in writing is that of Scardamalia (in press), and her analysis looked at only one aspect of processing load—the coordination of content schemes in expository writing. Even so, her findings are of considerable developmental interest. Among high-achieving children of ages 10 to 14, the treatment of content appears to be at a very low level of complexity. Children who are presumably capable of handling from three to five content schemes simultaneously tend in writing to manage only one to three. This would suggest that they are so hampered by low-order problems of getting language onto paper that they have little attentional capacity left over for higher order concerns with content.

A useful theory for interpreting the information-processing load aspects of writing is Pascual-Leone's theory of constructive operators (Pascual-Leone, 1970; Pascual-Leone & Goodman, 1976; Pascual-Leone & Smith, 1969). Of special importance as far as the analysis of writing abilities is concerned are two features of the theory: (1) it provides analytical methods that permit quantification of information load in the same terms over different kinds of task content (Bracewell, Scardamalia, & Bereiter, 1978); and (2) it brings under the same conceptual and analytical umbrella different ways that cognitive elements may secure a place in working memory. This second feature is important in explaining what would otherwise be anomalies in children's writing performance. Menig-Peterson and McCabe (1977) have observed that, although young children tend to produce incomplete and unfocused narratives under ordinary task instructions, they frequently produce complete and well-integrated narratives when stimulated to tell about an event of strong emotional import.

According to Pascual-Leone's theory, the principal limitation on the complexity of cognitive performance is the number of mental schemes that a person can keep simultaneously activated. A certain limited number can be kept active through mental effort—a number that increases with age, ranging from two to seven across the span of school years. But additional schemes may become activated because of emotional loading or because they are triggered by salient stimuli in the immediate environment. Thus it is that under facilitating emotional and stimulus conditions children can sometimes perform in ways characteristic of older children or adults (Odom, 1978; Odom, Cunningham, & Astor, 1975; Scardamalia, 1975). There is a tendency, as manifested in the Menig-Peterson and McCabe (1977) paper, and clearly traceable to the influence of Labov (1970), to treat the very best performance that can be elicited from children as defining the norm and to attribute everything else to experimental blundering or bias. When applied to a poorly understood phenomenon like writing behavior, such a view could seriously distort any normal developmental trends that might exist.

On the basis of the preceding considerations, we may state the following as a fundamental constraint on both the form and pace of writing development: Mature writing involves a large number of skills at different processing levels. Adequate mature functioning can be possible only when many of the skills are highly automated and when they are well enough coordinated to permit efficient time-sharing. Neither of these conditions is met in the young writer, and so the young writer, in order to function at all, must employ a structurally simpler system that does not require so much simultaneous and coordinated functioning. Since low-order schemes—those involved in getting words on to paper—must take priority in order for writing to occur, it follows that the system employed by the young writer must be one in which low-order schemes predominate and higher order schemes play a lesser part (Shuy, 1977). Movement toward a more complex system, in which higher order schemes predominate, would have to wait until the lower order schemes are sufficiently automatized.

At present there is not sufficient evidence by which to choose between a "gradualist" and a "structuralist" conception of writing development. A gradualist conception would hold simply that as low-order skills become automatized, higher order skills come into use. A structuralist conception would hold that the writing process, however it is carried out, has organization and that the incorporation of a new skill requires reorganization of the process. Accordingly, writing development will not be characterized simply by gradual elaboration and refinement of schemes at different processing levels but by more discrete stages of organization.

POSSIBLE STAGES IN WRITING DEVELOPMENT

Although a structuralist conception of writing development has a certain plausibility, it remains to construct a reasonable structural model—that is, a model that shows what successive structurally distinct stages of writing development might actually be like. A provisional model of this kind is advanced in this section. The word "stage" inevitably evokes the idea of Piagetian stages and all their associated conceptual baggage, but the word is used here with a more limited connotation. A stage is simply a *form of organization* that is preceded or followed by other forms. To suggest that there may be distinct stages in the development of writing abilities is not to suggest that those stages are universal or that they have a necessary order, much less that they are yoked to the Piagetian stages of cognitive development. The stages to be described here have a seemingly natural order to them, but it is quite conceivable that with a different sort of educational experience children might go through different stages with a different kind of order.

Six different systems of knowledge or skill may be identified in mature writing: fluency in producing written language, fluency in generating ideas, mastery of writing conventions, social cognition (appearing as ability to take account of the reader), literary appreciation and discrimination, and reflective thought. Each of these skill systems can develop, to a greater or lesser extent, independently of the others, and, of course, simultaneous development in all of them is to be expected across the span of school years. This does not mean, however, that all of these skill systems are involved in writing performance across the school years. Rather, it seems that writing development might follow a course similar in form to that which Schaeffer (1975) has described for development of number concepts.

Schaeffer (1975) calls his model of development "hierarchic skill integration." Because of children's information-processing capacity limitations, they cannot integrate all skills at once, as they would have to do in order to achieve something formally equivalent to mature performance. Instead, they integrate what skills they can in order to achieve a functional skill of a higher order. As this higher order skill becomes automatized, they integrate another skill with it to achieve yet a higher order skill, and so on. Applying this hierarchic concept to the six skill systems just mentioned, we get the picture of hierarchic skill integration shown in Fig. 4.1 and elaborated in the following sections.

Associative Writing.   The simplest system capable of producing intelligible writing is that which combines the two skill systems of fluency in written language and ideational fluency. The resulting skill of associative writing consists essentially of writing down whatever comes to mind, in the order in which it comes to mind. It is what Bobrow and Norman (1975) call a data-driven, as contrasted with a concept-driven, process. An empirical demonstration of such a process in writing comes from a study recently carried out by Brooks Masterton, Marlene Scardamalia, and the writer. Subjects were shown a picture by having masking pieces removed one at a time. Each exposure added significant new information. In describing the picture, the younger the subjects, the more likely they were to mention first what was newest to them as opposed to what would be most informative to a reader.

Much unskilled writing by students of all ages appears to be of this kind. One of the characteristics of "writer-based prose" noted by Flower (1979) in college students is that ideas are presented in the order they were acquired by the writer rather than in an order suited to the reader. The less talented grade 10 students whom we have interviewed even describe their writing as a process of putting down thoughts as they come to mind. Indeed, what they say about writing is much the same as what Keeney (1975) found with intermediate-grade children and Graves (1973) found with children at the very beginning of learning to write: Their principal obstacle is thinking of what to write. Given an "interesting" topic—that is, one that elicits an immediate flow of ideas—they can write easily and are pleased with what they produce. Self-chosen topics are, as one might expect, more likely to produce fluent ideation than are teacher-chosen ones. If the topic is "dull," then writing is difficult and the result, as judged by the students themselves, is a "dull" composition. This would follow from the data-driven character of the process. The associative writer lacks resources for creating an interesting composition. The same is true as regards coherence and completeness. Associative writers say they stop writing when they run out of ideas. If the topic is emotionally arousing enough that they need devote no

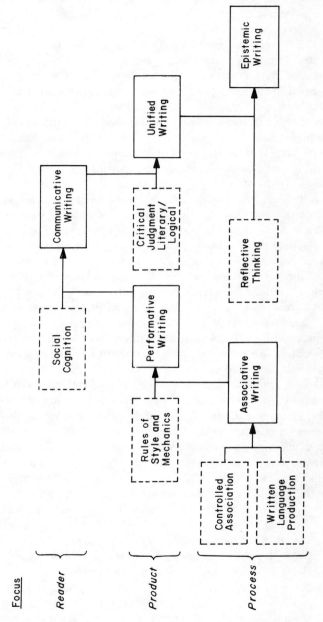

FIG. 4.1. A model of skill systems integration in writing development

mental effort to keeping the topic in mind, then their productions will tend to be unified and to appear fully developed and coherent. With less arousing topics, however, they are liable to lose hold and go off on a chain of associations irrelevant to the topic rather than produce associations that are all related to the topic (Scardamalia, in press).

Britton et al. (1975) recognize a similar early stage of writing that is relatively unplanned, uninhibited, unconcerned about audience reaction, and that is on the whole closer to transcribed speech than it is to literate writing. Their term for it is ''expressive'' writing. Expressive may appropriately describe the spontaneous writing of children, but it does not fit their more workaday efforts, which, however, display the same characteristics. When 10-year-olds were set the task of writing instructions for a game they had just learned, for instance (Scardamalia, Bereiter, & McDonald, 1977), many of them exhibited all the characteristics mentioned previously, but their writing could scarcely be called expressive.

The similarity of associative writing to transcribed speech may have an objective basis. Simon (1973) observed that children in the first years of schooling typically verbalize or subvocalize what they write, suggesting that they are in fact dictating to themselves. By the third year of school, this behavior had largely disappeared from the girls observed by Simon, and by the fourth year from the boys. This would suggest that by middle childhood the two skill systems of generating written language and controlled semantic association have become integrated into *associative writing*. Recent data that we have been collecting suggest, however, that this may be true only of narrative writing and that attainment of skillful associative writing comes much later for expository writing.

Performative Writing.   Most of traditional school writing instruction may be interpreted as an effort to shape students' associative writing into conformity with conventions of style and mechanics. This has proved to be a difficult instructional task. Although children may learn to spell and punctuate correctly in workbook and test exercises, thus demonstrating learning of these conventions, it remains a major step for them to incorporate this learning into their normal writing. The same is true for higher level conventions such as use of varied sentence patterns and avoidance of ambiguous reference. From the student's standpoint, concern about style and correctness disrupts the flow of associative writing. As one of our subjects put it (previously quoted by Scardamalia [in press]), ''I have all my thoughts in my mind but when I come to a word I can't spell it throws me off my writting [*sic*].''

What is here termed performative writing consists of the integration of associative writing with knowledge of stylistic conventions. It is reasonable to speak of this as a stage because it is a functional system actually achieved by many people—people who can, seemingly without conscious attention, produce writing that consists of well-formed standard English sentences, correctly spelled and punctuated. Performative writing is not, however, a stage in the sense of representing a single massive reorganization of behavior. Rather, it is clear that progress toward performative writing consists of a vast number of skill integrations, each requiring attention to a particular matter until it becomes an automatic part of writing behavior—the spelling of particular words, the punctuation of particular constructions, the use or avoidance of particular expressions, etc. (Shaughnessy, 1977). Thus it is that growth in the performative aspects of writing shows an overall continuity. But each particular skill integration imposes the same kind of cognitive demand on the learner—to attend simultaneously to the content of writing and to some feature of the emerging written product. Children's difficulties with revision—which is usually revision to bring the composition into closer conformity with conventions—undoubtedly also reflect this attentional capacity problem (Nold, in press).

Communicative Writing.   When performative writing is integrated with social cognition, the result is communicative writing—that is, writing that is calculated to have a desired effect on an audience. Britton et al. (1975) have used the term *transactional* to designate this kind of writing, contrasting it with *poetic*. In making this distinction, however, they limit the former kind of writing to what is more commonly known as expository writing. This categorization may be valid rhetorically: Clearly, different performative skills are involved in convincing or informing a reader from those that are involved in amusing or wringing tears from a reader. But from the standpoint of skill systems integration, they are all part of the same family.

Social cognition has a complex developmental history of its own (Looft, 1972; Shantz, 1976). Even toddlers appear capable of adapting messages to salient characteristics of intended receivers (Shatz & Gelman, 1973; Meissner & Apthorp, 1976). Yet under the difficult conditions of one-way communication to unobserved or unrevealing receivers, much older subjects behave as if they could not take the receiver's point of view into account (Flavell, 1977). It appears, then, that egocentric writing in middle childhood and beyond does not result from an absolute inability to take another person's point of view. Rather, it would seem that egocentric writing arises from an incapacity to take account of the reader and cope with all the other demands of writing at the same time (Scardamalia, in press). Because the other (associative and performative) demands are ordinarily preemptive, social cognition simply gets left out.

Although immature writers may be aware of reader-related requirements, this awareness appears able to affect their writing only in gross ways. Scardamalia, Bereiter, and McDonald (1977) had students write instructions for playing a novel game. When alerted, by means of a demonstration videotape, to the possibilities for miscommunication of game rules, the effect on younger (grade 4) students was simply to induce them to say more and thus to cover more points, but not to express particular points more clearly. In another instruction-writing experiment (Bracewell, Scardamalia, & Bereiter, 1978), reader saliency was varied from a condition in which no reader was specified to one in which the instructions were to be contained in a letter to a named unknown person, the letter sealed in an envelope, and addressed, with assurance that the letter would be delivered and a response returned. Subjects of all ages, from 10 to adult, showed a tendency to adapt messages more to their readers when they expected feedback as to results; but not until grade 12 did they show a significant tendency to adapt messages to the supposed level of sophistication of their readers.

Unified Writing.   The defining characteristic of this next stage of writing is that it takes account not only of other people's perspectives but of the writer's own perspective *as a reader*. As readers, children do more than acquire knowledge about how writing should be done, which serves them in performative writing. They also grow in ability to respond critically and esthetically to what they read. These evaluative skills are not automatically applied to their own writing, however. Implicit in the present model is the speculation that it is easier to take the point of view of another person (as in communicative writing) than it is to take the point of view of oneself as reader.

Once one is able to integrate one's own evaluative reading skills with one's writing skills, however, an important feedback loop is established. Writing comes to be shaped according to one's own standards, which in turn are shaped by what one has written. As a result the writer begins to develop a personal style and a personal viewpoint. Writing becomes more authentic and satisfying. One does not merely write to entertain the reader but also to please oneself. One does not argue simply to convince the reader but also to present an argument that oneself finds convincing. From a rhetorical standpoint, however, the most important consequence of the establishment of this writing-reading feedback loop is that it leads to a focus on the written product as a thing to be fashioned. Hence writing becomes a productive craft and not merely an instrumental skill.

Unified writing includes what Britton et al. (1975) call *poetic* writing and that they characterize as creating "a verbal construct, an 'object' made out of language [p. 90]." As noted previously, however, their categories are genre-related, whereas the present scheme deals with cognitive systems. Although writing a well-crafted story and writing a logically coherent argument may differ in the particular rhetorical skills they draw upon, they would appear to be alike in the kind of processing mechanism involved; both require the involvement of one's own critical capacities in a writing-reading feedback loop.

Epistemic Writing.   Writing probably always plays an epistemic function in that our knowledge gets modified in the process of being written down. The satisfaction that many children derive from writing about their personal experiences probably does not derive only from sharing the experiences but also from what Church (1961) calls *thematization*—the processing of experience into verbal form. As the capacity for reflective thought develops, however, writing can take on a more complex epistemic function (Nystrand & Widerspiel, 1977). Writing, because of its amenability to storage, review, and revision, makes possible a kind of extended and involved thought that is almost impossible without writing (Olson, 1977).

Epistemic writing emerges when the person's skill system for reflective thought is integrated with his skill system for unified writing. The creation of a literary work then becomes, in addition to whatever else it may be, a personal search for meaning. This seems to be what people mean by "serious" literature, as contrasted with literature that exists solely as "verbal artifact." (It should be clear, however, that epistemic writing is not limited to literature of ideas. A search for meaning could be carried out entirely through narrative imagery, for instance, without any propositional thought at all.) The teacher-student "process-conference" advocated by Graves (1978) appears to be aimed at helping students develop the epistemic potential of writing.

Epistemic writing represents the culmination of writing development, in that writing comes to be no longer merely a product of thought but becomes an integral part of thought. It becomes part of what Vygotsky has called the "extracortical organization of complex mental functions [quoted in Luria, 1973, p. 31]." As a result, the various skill systems that have been integrated to produce mature writing competence may now be enriched by the cognitive consequences of writing.

WRITING DEVELOPMENT AND SCHOOLING

The Schools Council research (Britton et al., 1975) illustrates the extent to which writing development, in a highly schooled society, is whatever the schools make it to be. Scribner and Cole (in press) show that in the rare case of the Vai, where a written language exists that is not mediated through schooling, writing is simply an adjunct to speaking and develops along with it. If writing were only what the schools make it, however, it is doubtful if anyone would get beyond the first two stages described in the preceding section. Traditional writing instruction, based on style manuals, models, and teacher correction, is almost wholly devoted to moving students from associative to performative writing. The alarm generated by the National Assessment of Educational Progress (1975) results and other less cogent findings has to do with the apparent failure of students to achieve performative writing, not with their failure to go beyond it.

Success in transcending or bypassing performative writing and moving students to higher stages is claimed for a number of innovative approaches, however. Several focus on communicative writing (Elsasser & John-Steiner, 1977; Pettigrew, Tefft, & Van Nostrand, 1977). The work of Kohl (1967) suggests that children who are not proficient at either performative or communicative writing may nevertheless undertake unified writing, in the sense of using writing to produce esthetically satisfying objects. Jacobs (1970) claimed success in moving elementary school children directly to epistemic writing, through what amounted to a behavior-shaping process. Epistemic writing appears also to be the goal of Elbow's (1973) unusual approach, designed for people who are "hung up" on performative writing. His freewriting technique evidently induces regression to associative writing, following which a dialectical process of working out thoughts in writing is pursued.

These divergent experiments support the view that has already been suggested several times in this chapter, that there is no natural order of writing development, in the sense of a fixed sequence that all writers must go through. At the same time, however, the experimental approaches suggest that it is at least meaningful to think of writing development in terms of discrete stages, each characterized by conscious focus on a particular aspect of writing. The stages may be ordered differently by different educational approaches, but they do not simply run together into amorphous growth.

It remains to be argued, however, that some orderings of stages may be more "natural" than others. In order to mount such an argument, it is necessary to distinguish sharply between mastery and automaticity. If mastery of one kind of writing had to be achieved before progress to a higher level kind of writing, then development would be impossible. Automaticity does not imply mastery but only proficiency such that the behavior in question requires little or no conscious attention. Examples of automaticity without mastery are to be found in people with fluent but illegible handwriting or with confident but inaccurate spelling. The preferred or "natural" order of writing development would be a sequence of stages in which the attainment of automaticity at one stage maximally facilitates progress toward the next stage.

The sequence of stages depicted in Fig. 4.1 would seem to be a "natural" order on these terms. The attainment of fluency in associative writing frees attentional capacity for dealing with performative demands. (Although concern with performative demands—that is, with meeting conventional standards of correctness in writing—may not be "natural," it is certainly consistent with the general readiness of children in the preadolescent years to be socialized to prevailing norms of rightness [Gesell, Ilg, & Ames, 1946].) Attaining a degree of mastery over stylistic conventions leads in turn to the discovery that writing can be used to affect the reader—that it can direct, inform, amuse, move emotionally, and so on. Thence emerges the communicative stage. Once students start writing for readers, it becomes a natural next step for them to start reading their own writing, which sets in motion the writing-reading feedback loop on which the stage of unified writing depends. Once this feedback loop is functioning well, it will be natural to discover that it leads not only to improved writing but also to improved understanding—that the loop constitutes a kind of dialogue with oneself. Thus may emerge the final, epistemic stage of writing development.

INDICATIONS FOR RESEARCH

One reason that speculations about writing development must be so tentative is that the available data mostly relate to what children *do* do under typical composition-writing circumstances and not to what they *can* do under maximally revealing circumstances. Chomsky (1964), noting the same condition in research on grammar in young children, pointed out the kinds of errors of interpretation that may result. Children may be wrongly judged to lack a certain competence simply because circumstances failed to elicit performance that would have revealed it. On the other hand, children may be wrongly judged to possess a certain competence on the basis of performance that is limited to the circumstances observed (e.g., a child might exhibit some formula expressions such as "He got run over by a truck" without having any general command of the passive transformation). Chomsky did not recommend any ways out of this predicament except broadly to suggest that "rather devious kinds of observations" would have to be made in different circumstances "so that a variety of evidence may be brought to bear on the attempt to determine what is in fact the underlying linguistic competence at each stage of development [p. 36]."

A parallel recommendation is clearly called for in writing research. Research based on "writing samples" collected under conditions more or less resembling those of typical classroom writing have served to give us a picture of what written language and composition are normally like at different ages. With conclusion of the definitive studies of Britton et al. (1975) and Loban (1976), it is likely that research of this kind has yielded about all that it can concerning the normal course of writing development. Further knowledge is more likely to come through the use of specialized tasks and other techniques that break through habitual school writing behaviors.

ACKNOWLEDGMENT

The writer wishes to thank Marlene Scardamalia for valuable suggestions and criticisms throughout the preparation of this chapter.

REFERENCES

Adams, M. J., & Collins, A. *A schema-theoretic view of reading comprehension.* ERIC Document No. ED 142 971, 1977.

Allen, R. L. *English grammars and English grammar.* New York: Scribner's, 1972.

Blount, N. S. Research on teaching literature, language and composition. In R. M. W. Travers (Ed.), *Second handbook of research on teaching.* Chicago: Rand-McNally, 1973.

Bobrow, D. G., & Norman, D. A. Some principles of memory schemata. In D. G. Bobrow & A. M. Collins (Eds.), *Representation and understanding: Studies in cognitive science.* New York: Academic Press, 1975.

Bracewell, R. J., Scardamalia, M., & Bereiter, C. *The development of audience awareness in writing.* Paper presented at the annual meeting of the American Educational Research Association, Toronto, March 1978. (ERIC Document Reproduction Service No. ED 154 433)

Braddock, R., Lloyd-Jones, R., & Schoer, L. *Research in written composition.* Champaign, Ill.: National Council of Teachers of English, 1963.

Britton, J., Burgess, T., Martin, N., McLeod, A., & Rosen, H. *The development of writing abilities (11-18).* London: Macmillan Education, Ltd., 1975.

Case, R. Gearing the demands of instruction to the developmental capacities of the learner. *Review of Educational Research,* 1975, *45*(1), 59-87.

Case, R. Implications of developmental psychology for the design of effective instruction. In A. M. Lesgold, J. W. Pellegrino, S. D. Fokemma, & R. Glaser (Eds.), *Cognitive psychology and instruction.* Plenum, N.Y.: Division of Plenum Publishing Corporation, 1978.

Chomsky, N. Formal discussion of "The development of grammar in child language" by W. Miller and S. Ervin. In U. Bellugi and R. Brown (Eds.), The acquisition of language. *Monographs of Society for Research in Child Development, 92,* Child Development Publications, 1964.

Church, J. *Language and the discovery of reality.* New York: Random House, 1961.

Collis, K. F., & Biggs, J. B. *Classroom examples of cognitive development phenomena.* ERDC Funded Project 7/41, University of Newcastle, undated.

Diebel, A., & Sears, I. A study of common mistakes in pupils' written English. *Elementary School Journal,* 1917, *18,* 172-185.

Elbow, P. *Writing without teachers.* London: Oxford University Press, 1973.

Elsasser, N., & John-Steiner, V. P. An interactionist approach to advancing literacy. *Harvard Educational Review,* 1977, *47,* 355-369.

Emig, J. *The composing processes of twelfth graders* (Research Report No. 13). Champaign, Ill.: National Council of Teachers of English, 1971.

Flavell, J. H. *Cognitive development.* Englewood Cliffs, N.J.: Prentice-Hall, 1977.

Flower, L. Writer-based prose: A cognitive basis for problems in writing. *College English,* 1979, *41,* 19-37.

Fodor, J. A. Bever, T. G., & Garrett, M. F. *The psychology of language: An introduction to psycholinguistics and generative grammar.* New York: McGraw-Hill, 1974.

Gesell, A. L., Ilg, F. L., & Ames, L. B. *The child from five to ten.* New York: Harper & Bros., 1946.

Gleason, H. A., Jr. *Linguistics and English grammar.* New York: Holt, Rinehart & Winston, 1965.

Goody, J., & Watt, I. The consequences of literacy. *Comparative Studies in Society and History,* 1963, *5,* 304-345.

Graves, D. H. *Children's writing: Research directions and hypotheses based upon an examination of the writing process of seven-year-old children.* Unpublished doctoral dissertation, State University of New York at Buffalo, 1973.

Graves, D. H. *Balance the basics: Let them write.* New York: Ford Foundation, 1978.

Havelock, E. A. Prologue to Greek literacy. In C. Boulter (Ed.), *Lectures in memory of Louise Taft Semple, second series.* Cincinnati: University of Oklahoma Press for the University of Cincinnati, 1973.

Hill, J. D. *An analysis of the writing of elementary children, grades 2 through 6, to determine the presence, frequency of use and development by grade level of specified literary devices.* Unpublished doctoral dissertation, Indiana University, 1972.

Hunt, J. M. Piaget's observations as a source of hypotheses concerning motivation. *Merrill-Palmer Quarterly of Behavior and Development,* 1963, *9*(4), 263-276.

Jacobs, G. H. L. *When children think.* New York: Teachers College Press, Columbia University, 1970.

Keeney, M. L. *An investigation of what intermediate-grade children say about the writing of stories.* Unpublished doctoral dissertation, Lehigh University, 1975.

Klahr, D., & Wallace, J. G. *Cognitive development: An information-processing view.* Hillsdale, N.J.: Lawrence Erlbaum Associates, 1976.

Kohl, H. *Thirty-six children.* New York: Signet Books, 1967.

Labov, W. *The study of nonstandard English.* Champaign, Ill.: National Council of Teachers of English (by special arrangement with the Center for Applied Linguistics, 1970).

Loban, W. D. *The language of elementary school children* (Research Report No. 1). Urbana, Ill.: National Council of Teachers of English, 1963.

Loban, W. D. *Problems in oral English* (Research Report No. 5). Urbana, Ill.: National Council of Teachers of English, 1966.

Loban, W. D. *Language development: Kindergarten through grade twelve* (Research Report No. 18). Urbana, Ill.: National Council of Teachers of English, 1976.

Long, R. B. *The sentence and its parts: A grammar of contemporary English.* Chicago: University of Chicago Press, 1961.

Looft, W. R. Egocentrism and social interaction across the life span. *Psychological Bulletin,* 1972, *78*(2), 73–92.

Luria, A. R. *The working brain: An introduction to neuropsychology.* London: Penguin Books, 1973.

Lyman, R. L. Summary of investigations relating to grammar, language and composition. Chicago: University of Chicago, 1929. (Supplementary Educational Monographs, No. 36, published in conjunction with *The School Review* and *The Elementary School Journal.*)

Meissner, J. A., & Apthorp, H. Nonegocentrism and communication mode switching in black preschool children. *Developmental Psychology,* 1976, *12*(3), 245–249.

Menig-Peterson, C., & McCabe, A. *Structure of children's narratives.* Paper presented at the biennial meetings of the Society for Research in Child Development, New Orleans, March 1977.

Moscovici, S., & Plon, M. Les situations-colloques: Observations theoriques et experimentales. *Bulletin de Psychologie,* 1966, *19*, 702–722.

National Assessment of Educational Progress. *Writing mechanics, 1966–1974: A capsule description of changes in writing mechanics* (Report No. 05. W-01). Denver, Colorado: National Assessment of Educational Progress, 1975.

Nold, E. W. Revising. In C. H. Frederiksen, M. S. Whiteman, & J. F. Dominic (Eds.), *Writing: The nature, development, and teaching of written communication.* Hillsdale, N.J.: Lawrence Erlbaum Associates, in press.

Nystrand, M. *Assessing written communicative competence: A textual cognition model.* Toronto: The Ontario Institute for Studies in Education, 1977. (ERIC Document Reproduction Service No. ED 133 732)

Nystrand, M., & Widerspiel, M. Case study of a personal journal: Notes towards an epistemology of writing. In M. Nystrand (Ed.), *Language as a way of knowing: A book of readings.* Toronto: The Ontario Institute for Studies in Education, 1977.

Odom, R. D. A perceptual-salience account of décalage relations and developmental change. In C. J. Brainerd & L. S. Siegel (Eds.), *Alternatives to Piaget: Critical essays on the theory.* New York: Academic Press, 1978.

Odom, R. D., Cunningham, J. G., & Astor, E. C. Adults thinking the way we think children think, but children don't always think that way: A study of perceptual salience and problem solving. *Bulletin of the Psychonomic Society,* 1975, *6*, 545–548.

O'Donnell, R. C., Griffin, W. J., & Norris, R. C. *Syntax of kindergarten and elementary school children: A transformational analysis* (Research Report No. 8). Champaign, Ill.: National Council of Teachers of English, 1967.

Olson, D. R. From utterance to text: The bias of language in speech and writing. *Harvard Educational Review,* 1977, *47*(3), 257–281.

Pascual-Leone, J. A mathematical model for the transition rule in Piaget's developmental stages. *Acta Psychologica,* 1970, *63*, 301–345.

Pascual-Leone, J., & Goodman, D. *Intelligence and experience: A neo-Piagetian approach.* Unpublished manuscript, York University, 1976.

Pascual-Leone, J., & Smith, J. The encoding and decoding of symbols by children: A new experimental paradigm and neo-Piagetian model. *Journal of Experimental Child Psychology,* 1969, *8,* 328–355.

Pettigrew, J., Tefft, N. E., & Van Nostrand, A. D. *Functional writing: Secondary school edition.* Providence, R.I.: Center for Research in Writing, 1977.

Posner, M., & Keele, S. W. Skill learning. In R. M. W. Travers (Ed.), *Second handbook of research on teaching.* Chicago: Rand-McNally, 1973.

Scardamalia, M. Two formal operational tasks: A quantitative neo-Piagetian and task analysis model for investigating sources of task difficulty. In G. I. Lubin, J. F. Magary, & M. K. Poulsen (Eds.), *Piagetian theory and its implications for the helping professions.* Los Angeles: University of Southern California Publications, 1975.

Scardamalia, M. How children cope with the cognitive demands of writing. In C. H. Frederiksen, M. S. Whiteman, & J. F. Dominic (Eds.), *Writing: The nature, development, and teaching of written communication.* Hillsdale, N.J.: Lawrence Erlbaum Associates, in press.

Scardamalia, M., Bereiter, C., & McDonald, J. D. S. *Role-taking in written communication investigated by manipulating anticipatory knowledge.* Paper presented at the biennial meeting of the Society for Research in Child Development, New Orleans, March 1977. (ERIC Document Reproduction Service No. ED 151 792)

Schaeffer, B. Skill integration during cognitive development. In A. Kennedy & A. Wilkes (Eds.), *Studies in long term memory.* London: John Wiley & Sons, 1975.

Scribner, S., & Cole, M. Unpackaging literacy. In C. H. Frederiksen, M. S. Whiteman, & J. F. Dominic (Eds.), *Writing: The nature, development, and teaching of written communication.* Hillsdale, N.J.: Lawrence Erlbaum Associates, in press.

Shantz, C. U. The development of social cognition. In E. M. Hetherington (Ed.), *Review of child development research* (Vol. 5). Chicago: University of Chicago Press, 1976.

Shatz, M., & Gelman, R. The development of communication skills: Modifications in the speech of young children as a function of the listener. *Monographs of the Society for Research in Child Development,* 1973, *38,* (5, Serial No. 152).

Shaughnessy, M. P. *Errors and expectations: A guide for the teacher of basic writing.* New York: Oxford University Press, 1977.

Shuy, R. W. *Toward a developmental theory of writing: Tapping and knowing.* Paper presented at National Institute of Education Conference on Writing, Los Alamitos, Calif., June 1977.

Simon, H. A. On the development of the processor. In S. Farnham-Diggory (Ed.), *Information processing in children.* New York: Academic Press, 1972.

Simon, H. A. How big is a chunk? *Science,* 1974, *183,* 482–488.

Simon, J. *La langue ecrite de l'enfant.* Paris: Presses Universitaires de France, 1973.

Stahl, A. Structual analysis of children's compositions. *Research in the Teaching of English,* 1974, *8,* 184–205.

Stahl, A. The structure of children's compositions: Developmental and ethnic differences. *Research in the Teaching of English,* 1977, *11,* 156–163.

Stallard, C. K. An analysis of the writing behavior of good student writers. *Research in the Teaching of English,* 1974, *8,* 206–218.

West, W. W. Written composition. *Review of Educational Research,* 1967, *37*(2), 159–167.

II WRITING RESEARCH AND APPLICATION

5 Experiments on Composing Letters: Some Facts, Some Myths, and Some Observations

John D. Gould
IBM, T. J. Watson Research Center

This chapter has two purposes: to summarize our experimental results on different methods of composition, and to provide some theoretical comments on composition stimulated by these and related experiments and speculations.

SUMMARY OF EXPERIMENTAL STUDIES

Introduction

This book is mainly concerned with writing. Our experiments have studied writing as well as dictating to a machine, typewriting using a computer-based text editor, and speaking. Speaking differs from dictating in that the author assumes the recipient will listen rather than read what has been composed, and the author need not give typing instructions.

A main motivation in studying composition was to develop some understanding of this pervasive, time-consuming psychological process that apparently takes years to master, if indeed it is mastered. A second motivation was to identify how technological systems could help improve composition. Our research strategy has been to vary the input tasks to authors and output (composition) methods of authors in order to identify and understand cognitive processes in composition. Input tasks have been varied by requiring participants to compose particular types of letters. We have used over 100 different letter assignments, ranging from simple messages to relatively complex "one-page" letters. Participants are videotaped while they compose, and the results are analyzed into the subprocesses of planning, generating, reviewing, and accessing additional information through reading or listening. In most experiments participants were told which composition method (e.g., writing, dictating) to use on each letter, although in a few experiments participants were given a choice of methods. An "experiment" typically consists of about 10 participants, each of whom composes several letters, one or more with each method being studied. About 20 experiments have been completed.

Methodological Issues in Getting Started

There is relatively little theoretical understanding of human production or generation, e.g., singing, whistling, writing, programming, drawing, compared to human perception. In part this is due to lack of experimental strategies and methodology for studying production tasks and, as a consequence, a lack of key experimental findings. This lack was evident when we began studying production tasks about a decade ago, e.g., text editing (Boies & Gould, 1970), programming (Boies & Gould, 1974; Gould & Drongowski, 1974), generating questions using query languages (Gould & Ascher, 1975; Thomas & Gould, 1975), composing instructions (Gould, Lewis, & Becker, 1976). Because of this, we faced several methodological issues in starting experimental studies of composition.

Methods of Composition.   Should we study writing only? Most people compose through writing, although some people dictate, either to a machine or secretary, or type their letters, memos, reports. We chose to study several methods of composition because we wanted to learn how much people's performance was determined by the particular method itself and how much it was determined by other, more general, central processes.

Individual Differences.   That people are different is certainly the first law of psychology. Should we study children, students, famous authors? So far our population of interest has been the millions of "white-collar" workers. We have studied about 50 adult college graduates, 20–65 years old. Included have been two groups who can be considered as experts at *particular methods* of composition—one group at dictating and one group at using computer-based text editors.

_ *Lab Experiments versus Field Study.*   Should people be observed as they compose their own documents (letters, memos, reports) or should laboratory experiments be conducted? We chose the latter primarily for control reasons, being cognizant of the artificial conditions that this can foster (discussed later under "Generalization Issues").

Micro-Tasks or Macro-Tasks.   Should we require participants to perform micro-tasks, so typical of experimental psychology? We considered a micro-task for studying planning, in part because of related studies (Goldman-Eisler, 1961; Rochester, 1973) and in part because we had developed advanced measurement techniques. One idea was to measure the position and duration of pauses when participants were requested to generate, with various methods, a clause, sentence, or longer description of a stimulus. Instead, however, we chose to study a larger part of the composition process. A participant comes to our laboratory and is given a description of a letter to compose. In most experiments participants are told which method of composition to use on each letter, although in a few experiments participants have been given a choice of composition method.

Complexity of Documents.   What type of documents should be studied? So far we have studied ''one-page'' letters and memos, which are the most prevalent form of composition. We have used over 100 different letter assignments, ranging from simple messages to relatively complex ''one-page'' letters. Examples include routine replies to information requests, letters of recommendation and application, summaries of daily activities, short essays on personal feelings, sales letters, letters of inquiry, and letters planning events. Without developing a formal taxonomy of the difficulty of the letter assignments, we have attempted to understand psychological processes in ''easy'' and ''hard'' one-page letters.

Independent Variables.   What variables are of most interest? The main one we have studied is methods of composition. Besides providing basic data on each method, this identifies the similarities and differences in the psychological processes involved. ''Experts'' versus ''novices'' have been studied in dictation. Letter complexity, although not varied systematically, has also been studied. Certainly composition strategies are important to study, and we have begun studying this through varying the speed/quality emphasis in instructions to participants.

Dependent Variables.   What should be measured? Participants' *performance* and their *attitude and beliefs* about it have both been measured. Participants are videotaped while composing, and the videotapes are analyzed into component performance times. To do this, *composition* time—i.e., from when a participant begins reading the description of the letter to be composed until it is finished—is divided into several subtimes. *Generating* (actual speaking, dictating, writing, or typing) was initially analyzed by replaying the tapes several times. Now we have apparatus, designed with Alfonso Quinones, IBM Research Scientific Services, that automatically detects generating times and pause times (Gould & Quinones, 1978). *Reviewing* and *Accessing Information* through reading or listening are analyzed by replaying the videotapes. *Planning* is usually analyzed from the remaining pauses. Details of editing are obtained by replaying the videotapes.

Letter quality has been measured after each experiment in several ways. Judges have rated it in various areas, e.g., syntax, grammar, format, effectiveness, style. On other occasions, judges have been asked to select the most effective letters submitted in various "contests," e.g., nominating a favorite teacher. Judges have also been asked to pick out, from typed versions of letters on the same subject, the dictated ones and the written ones.

Attitudes and beliefs have been measured in several ways. For example, we have attempted to understand the criteria authors use in judging their own work by having them rate their own compositions from several points of view. Authors have also rated the quality of their compositions at different stages. In other experiments, authors have predicted the method of composition they would use under various circumstances, and then later we have recorded what they actually chose under such circumstances.

Fixed Variables.   There are many variables which presumably could affect the results, which we have not yet been able to study systematically. One of these is the strategies that, through instruction, participants are encouraged to adopt. Should they use a "spew" strategy in which they quickly generate a first draft, and then revise several later versions? Or should they adopt a "first-time" final strategy, in which they aim to make the first draft the final draft? We adopted the latter, in part because word-processing centers in offices today often require this. In retrospect, this choice was probably realistic, given the fact that many authors do little revising anyway (see Bracewell, Scardamalia, & Bereiter, 1978; Scardamalia, in press; Stallard, 1974, for results on high school and college students). In most experiments described here, participants were required to compose formal letters, including a return address, inside address, salutation, body, and closing. A secretary typed the written and dictated letters. A decision related to this was to allow one proof-editing session, or later redo of a letter. Another related decision was that the typist was to act as a "good secretary," but not do any revising or correct misspelled words or incorrect grammar.

Generalization Issues.   To what population and to what types of documents can we generalize? We have been especially concerned with this because of our applied interest. In terms of the letter assignments, we have required participants to compose letters on subject matter with which they would be familiar. School situations provide many good opportunities. But we have been careful that the letters have a general business tone to them so that they will also relate to office communications. At another level, we have been careful that our statistics generalize not only to other people beyond those studied, but also to other letters beyond those specifically studied (see Clark, 1973).

Initial Hypotheses

Because of the lack of experimental work done in this area in the past, we started with several intuitive hypotheses:

1. Dictating requires a long time to learn.
2. Eventually, dictating is much faster than writing. That is, potential maximum output rates, as measured informally, are 200 words per minute (wpm) and 40 wpm, respectively (Gould, 1979).
3. Dictating may be qualitatively superior to writing because the higher potential output rate permits faster transfer of ideas from limited capacity working memory, thus reducing forgetting through interference or decay.
4. Speaking may be more "natural" than dictating (or writing). Authors may use a syntax and phraseology that they have learned over the years that is appropriate for listening, but may not be appropriate for reading. In addition, in contrast to dictation, authors do not have to give typing instructions, which is potentially a disruptive "secondary" task.
5. Writing has an advantage over dictating because it is easier to review and modify.

Key Results

Learning to Dictate. Does it take a long time to learn to dictate as well as one writes? No. Eight college graduates who had never dictated before spent part of one day learning to dictate to a machine. They returned the next day, and, among other tasks, wrote by hand two routine business letters and two more complex letters, and dictated two routine business letters and two more complex letters. Routine letters were replies to requests for information. Complex letters included "one-page essays" on capital punishment, the Bicentennial, and an outstanding teacher.

Table 5.1 (data from Gould, 1978a) shows that they dictated letters and wrote letters in about the same time and with about the same quality. Quality was rated by judges afterward on a 5-point scale, where 1 = Unacceptable, 3 = Acceptable, and 5 = Exceptional. Participants made few changes, either during composition or during subsequent proof-editing of the typed copy.

Years of Practice. How much faster does one get with years of additional practice at composition? We tested this for dictation. Eight "expert" dictators, business executives who have dictated regularly for years and preferred dictating to writing, went through the same experiments.

Table 5.2 (data from Gould, 1978c) shows that these "expert" dictators dictated routine business letters about 20% faster than did the novice dictators (but $p > .05$), and they dictated the more complex letters in the same time as did the novice dictators. They spent somewhat more time writing than did the novices, however. The quality of both groups' work was rated as acceptable after the experiment. Dictated and written letters were similar. Judges were slightly better than chance at selecting the typed versions of dictated letters from the

TABLE 5.1
Composition Times (Min) and Judged Quality by Novice Dictators[a]
(Data from Gould, 1978a)

Method	Routine Business Letters		More Complex Letters	
	Time (Min)	Quality	Time (Min)	Quality
Writing	6.4	3.2	11.2	3.2
Dictating	5.7	2.9	10.2	3.1

[a] Quality was based on a 5-point scale where 1 = Unacceptable, 3 = Acceptable, and 5 = Excellent.

typed versions of written letters. The difference between the two groups on the routine letters was because the experienced dictators, compared to the inexperienced dictators, spent somewhat less time pausing and reviewing. Generation times and generation rates were the same for both groups.

Compared to themselves, expert dictators dictated the routine business letters about 60% faster than they themselves wrote them, and they dictated the more complex letters about 20% faster than they themselves wrote them (Table 5.2).

Thus, although years of experience may result in faster dictation than writing, it is far below the 400–500% difference that one might expect on the basis of potential output rates. The reason is that planning time, as inferred primarily from pauses (Gould, 1978a, 1978c, 1979), was two-thirds of composition time. Assuming planning time is not affected by output method (an assumption that is not entirely correct, as discussed later), then a fast output method can have only a limited effect upon total composition time.

Secondary Tasks.   Do "secondary tasks," such as operating equipment and giving typing instructions, decrease one's dictation performance? Pilot experiments and self-reports of novice dictators indicated that, after the training day of dictation practice, they do not. Thus, the planned formal study of these secondary tasks was not completed.

TABLE 5.2
Dictation Times (Min) by Novice and Expert Dictators[a]

	Routine Business Letters		More Complex Letters	
	Writing	Dictating	Writing	Dictating
Novices	6.4	5.7	11.2	10.2
Experts	7.1	4.6	12.9	10.2

[a] From Gould, 1978a, and Gould, 1978c. (Gould, 1978c, copyright 1978 by the American Psychological Association. Reprinted by permission.)

What Gets Learned. How does performance change as one first learns a composition method? We studied this question for dictation. During the training day, novice dictators became faster at dictating a series of 10 similar, simple business letters (Table 5.3 from Gould, 1978a): 4.6 min on each of the first two letters versus 2.8 min on each of the last two letters, F (9,63) = 3.14, p < .01). The improvement was caused mainly by a decrease in pauses and reviews, and more frequent overlapping of generating (actual dictating) with reading. (This effect, where participants initially perform related parts of a complex task serially but begin overlapping them with practice, is observed in many learning situations, e.g., learning to do arithmetic operations, drive a car, adapt to displaced vision, program a computer.) Faster generation rates (in wpm) were only a secondary consideration.

Invisible Writing. Writing provides a more easily reviewed and modified external record of what one has just composed than does dictating or speaking. To test how important this is, we had participants compose letters in "invisible writing." They wrote with a wooden stylus on a sheet of paper that had a carbon paper and another sheet of paper underneath it. Thus, participants could not see what they wrote, although a permanent record was produced. Table 5.4 (data from Gould, 1978a) shows that the time, quality, and number of proof-editing changes were the same for writing, invisible writing, and dictating, on both routine letters and more complex letters. Similar results were found with the experienced dictators, i.e., business executives (Gould, 1978c). As already mentioned, participants spent little time reviewing their dictating or writing, and in all three methods they made few changes, either while composing or in subsequent proof-editing. This explains the similar composition times and the lack

TABLE 5.3
Times (Min) and Judged Quality on Ten Similar, Simple Business
Letters for Novice Dictators Just Learning to Dictate[a]
(Data from Gould, 1978a)

	1st, 2nd Letters	9th, 10th Letters
Composition Time (Min)	4.6	2.5[b] (p < .01)
Generation Time (Min)	1.6	1.2 (p < .05)
Pause Time (Min)	1.6	0.6 (p < .05)
Review Time (Min)	1.0	0.2
Quality Rating	2.8	3.2 (p < .01)

[a] Quality was based on a 5-point scale where 1 = Unacceptable, 3 = Acceptable, and 5 = Excellent.

[b] The component times do not sum to the total time because a few videotapes were missing and others had to be substituted for these component time analyses.

TABLE 5.4
Composition Times, Proof-Editing Changes, Quality, and Median Ranking
(out of sets of 8 letters on the same topic)
(Data from Gould, 1978a)[a]

Method	Composition Time	Proof-Editing Changes	Mean Quality Rating	Median Quality Ranking
Writing	11.2	Few	3.2	4th
Invisible Writing	9.8	Few	3.0	4th
Dictating	10.2	Few	3.1	4th

[a] Quality was based on a 5-point scale where 1 = Unacceptable, 3 = Acceptable, and 5 = Excellent.

of a reduction in quality with invisible writing. Although participants' performance was not affected, they clearly did not like invisible writing and would not use it in the real world.

Speaking.   Speaking letters may be more "natural" than dictating them (or writing them). Flower (1979) has suggested that many writers actually say to themselves what they are about to write, often having difficulty translating this acceptable internal speech (which mimics external speech) into acceptable written constructions. In several experiments, we have found that speaking is faster than dictating (and writing), at least on routine letters (Gould & Boies, 1978b), as shown in Table 5.5 (data from Gould, 1978a, 1978c). These initial experiments may have inadvertently reduced potential differences between speaking and other methods, as participants sometimes did not always differentiate between dictating and speaking.

In additional experiments that avoid these problems (Gould, 1978c) participants assumed that their written letters were to be read directly by recipients (they would not be typed) and their spoken letters would be heard by recipients. Figure

TABLE 5.5
Composition Times (Min) for Eight Novice Dictators and
Eight Experienced Dictators (in parentheses)[a]

	Routine Letters	Complex Letters
Writing	6.4 (7.1)	11.2 (12.9)
Dictating	5.7 (4.6)	10.2 (10.2)
Speaking	3.5 (3.6)	8.8 (10.0)

[a] Data for novice dictators are from Gould, 1978a, and data for experienced dictators are from Gould, 1978c. (Gould, 1978c, copyright by the American Psychological Association. Reprinted by permission.)

5.1 shows two key results from four of these experiments. Twelve participants wrote one or more letters and spoke one or more letters in each experiment. The experiments differed in letter complexity. Participants composed routine letters in Experiment 1, more complex letters in Experiments 2 and 3, and short messages in Experiment 4.

First, speaking was generally 35%–75% faster than writing—even though participants had no previous experience at noninteractive speaking. This difference between speaking and writing is greater than the difference between dictating and writing—even for experienced dictators (Table 5.5). Speaking may be faster than dictating because composing an oral letter to be read rather than heard may require extra time. This could be due to unfamiliarity, multiple audiences (the secretary and the recipient), or the requirement to use grammar and syntax suitable for reading. Alternatively, a person may just talk more slowly when a listener must type what is said.

Second, planning time was not a constant *amount* for both methods, as shown by the cross-hatched bars of Fig. 5.1. Rather it was a constant *ratio*, i.e., two-thirds of composition time, regardless of method or type of letter. Although written letters tended to be 20% longer than spoken letters, there were no other gross qualitative differences between them.

What Participants Think of Their Compositions.   The time and quality of participants' *performance* showed relatively small differences in different methods of composition. Do participants *think* that they perform the same with different methods of composition? In experiments addressing this question, participants rated their compositions at three stages: first, just after composing each letter; second, about 30–60 min later, after receiving a typed version and incor-

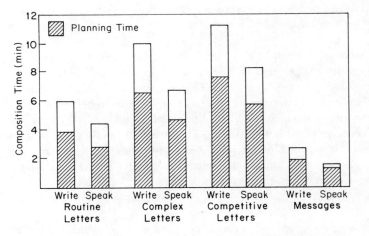

FIG. 5.1   Planning time as affected by composition (output) method.

porating any proof-editing changes; and, third, 2 weeks later. Table 5.6 (data from Gould & Boies, 1978a) shows the results for writing and dictating from one experiment. The answer is "yes" for novice dictators and "no" for experienced dictators. Novice dictators, just after composing them, rated their dictated letters as significantly poorer than their written letters, but subsequently rated them as equivalent. Experienced dictators, on the other hand, rated their written and dictated letters as equivalent at all stages. Few proof-editing changes were made at Stage 2 by either group with either method. (Another experiment, Gould & Boies [1978a] showed similar results, except that novice dictators did not rate their writing and dictating as equivalent until the third stage.) This poor, and unrealistic, evaluation by novices of their dictation may be one reason (among many) that they do not dictate.

Communication Effectiveness.   In experiments described so far, participants' performance was judged on the basis of speed and quality. But in real life, communications are judged primarily on how well they communicate, i.e., how effective they are at modifying a recipient's knowledge, judgment, understanding, or point of view. This is the goal of communications. To measure this type of effectiveness, 12 participants composed letters for competitive situations (Gould, 1979): in one letter, each acted as a representative of a paper company trying to win a customer's bid for an order, and in the other each nominated his or her favorite teacher for an award. They were told judges would afterward select the winner in each contest. Half the participants wrote the sales letter and spoke the teacher letter, whereas the other half did the opposite. The results showed no differential effect of writing versus speaking. Of the three winners in each contest (actually three letters tied for second place in one contest), four were spoken and three were written. The key result was that the three winning authors of one contest were among the four winners of the other contest. Thus, again differences among authors were more important than differences among methods here.

Annotating.   Frequently one makes annotations or comments on documents, usually written comments on printed documents. In principle, one could also make spoken comments on printed documents, and make written or spoken comments on audio documents. We have explored the relationships among these four conditions in a task in which 12 participants assumed they were editors of a local news service (Gould, 1979). The strongest result was not participants' performance but their preferences. Nine participants preferred making written comments on printed material. Quite consistently, participants next preferred making spoken comments on printed material, followed by making written comments on audio material, and spoken comments on audio material.

Choosing a Method.   Do people accurately predict which method of composition they will use under various circumstances? No. After 12 participants had

TABLE 5.6
Composition Times (Min), Authors' Own Ratings at Three Stages,
and Other Authors' Ratings[a]

	Composition Time (Min)	Author's 1 Rating	Author's 2 Rating	Author's 3 Rating	Ratings by Other Participants
Novices					
Write	8.4	4.4	4.5	3.9	3.6
Dictate	8.5	3.8	4.6	4.1	3.6
Experts					
Write	12.9	4.4	4.8	4.5	3.6
Dictate	10.2	4.3	4.5	4.5	3.9

[a] Ratings were made on a 7-point scale, where 1 = Unacceptable, 4 = Acceptable, and 7 = Excellent.

spent half a day composing written letters and spoken letters, they filled out a brief questionnaire (Gould, 1979). (They did this before they knew that later they would actually choose either method when composing an additional series of letters.) Eleven of them said they would *write* if they "wanted highest quality" or "were trying to be most effective." The 12th person showed no preference. Eleven said they would *speak* if they "were in a hurry." The 12th participant's answer was not clear. Table 5.7 shows the results. Eight participants selected speaking when they had to compose four very brief messages.

In tasks in which each participant composed three routine letters, six were given speed instructions and six were given quality instructions. The results somewhat followed what participants said they would do. Speaking was selected

TABLE 5.7
Number of Times Each Method Was Actually Selected in
Three Different Tasks by Twelve Participants[a]
(Data from Gould, 1979)

Task	Brief Messages	Routine Letters		Complex Letters	
Motivation		Speed	Quality	Speed	Quality
Method					
Writing	16	5	12	9	7
Speaking	32	13	6	3	5

[a] In the Message Task, each participant composed 4 messages, using either W or S. In the Routine Letter Task, six participants received Speed instructions and six received Quality instructions. Each composed 3 letters. In the Complex Letter Task, each participant received the opposite instructions from the Routine Letter Task. Each composed 2 letters.

for 13 of 18 letters composed under speed instructions, and writing was selected for 12 of 18 letters composed under quality instructions. In a third task participants composed two "more complex" letters, and the instructions were reversed for each participant. Here the method actually chosen was very different from what participants said they would choose. Seven of 12 letters were written under quality instructions, but 9 of 12 were written under speed instructions! Participants said they chose to write these complex letters under speed instructions because of familiarity and comfort with writing and the expectation that "better letters" would ultimately be produced faster by writing than by speaking.

Limiting Factors in Composition.   These results show that output modality in composition is not the limiting factor. Composition rates (total words/time to compose a letter) were typically 13 wpm for writing, 23 wpm for dictating, and 30 wpm for speaking (Gould, 1978a, 1979).

Our initial studies (Gould, 1978a, 1978c) reported that generation rates (total words/generation time) were considerably less than maximum possible rates, i.e., being one-half the maximum 40 wpm for writing, generally less than one-fourth the maximum 200 wpm for dictating—regardless of experience, and one-third the maximum 200 wpm for speaking. These results showed that generation rates were at least twice as great in dictation and speaking as in writing. Since then we have developed much more precise measurement techniques that show that generation rates are a function of the precision of analysis. By measuring every generation longer than 100 msec and not including in generation time any pause longer than 100 msec, generation rates are about 40 wpm for writing and 100–125 wpm for speaking (Gould, 1979).

The main factor in composition is planning time, which is two-thirds of composition time.

Similarities Among Methods.   Although in many ways the aim has been to find differences among methods of composition, many similarities have been found. Planning time was two-thirds of composition time, regardless of method (Gould, 1978a, 1978c, 1979). Composition rates for a given method were usually not much affected by apparent difficulty of the letters. (In everyday life this result undoubtedly has limits, e.g., a one-page letter applying for a new job versus an informal note to a friend.) Good authors were good authors and poor authors were poor authors, regardless of method. At a more detailed level, in all methods, participants generally overlapped reading routine external information (e.g., an inside address) and generating it (e.g., copying or speaking it). They usually made a long pause around the salutation of a letter and began planning the body. They rarely made notes. They reviewed infrequently, briefly, and locally. They made few changes, either during composition (or during subsequent proof-editing). When they did make changes, they were usually "immediate" (i.e., just after writing, dictating, or speaking the "mistake") rather than "de-

layed.'' These changes were also ''local'' (i.e., where an author had just generated) rather than global, and consisted of one or two words. No gross differences
were found in the style of a given author among the various methods of letters.
Letters generally had the same average sentence length (18–19 words in one set
of experiments). Written and dictated letters were very similar. Judges performed
only slightly better than chance when required to select blindly typed versions of
dictated letters from typed versions of written letters.

Differences Among Authors.   One might assume that some authors are relatively better at writing and other authors are relatively better at dictating or
speaking. However, results strongly suggest that good authors (on the basis of
time and quality) are good authors, regardless of composition method, and poor
authors are poor authors (Gould, 1978c, 1979). Variance among participants is
greater than variance among methods (Gould, 1978c).

Skill.   Is dictation a ''skill''? (Or, for that matter, is speaking letters a
''skill''?) Skilled performance is usually assumed to consist of a number of
components or subskills, to be organized at several intricately interlinked levels,
to involve generally a motor component (but perhaps also heavily involve cognition), and to show large learning effects, oftentimes over months or years.
During skill acquisition obvious problem-solving and search behaviors disappear
and performance appears automatic and routine. Once a subskill has become
automatic, cognitive attention is no longer required and can be allocated elsewhere, including to the acquisition of other components or subskills, to their
integration, and to deeper levels of processing. There are large quantitative and
qualitative differences between a skilled performer and a novice. (For relevant
discussion of skill, see Bartlett, 1958; LaBerge & Samuels, 1974; Card, Moran,
& Newell, 1976; Miller & Johnson-Laird, 1976.)

Although dictation may fulfill some of these criteria, it does not fulfill the
most observable ones. Learning by novices was rapid (a few hours at most),
problem-solving behaviors related to dication per se were nearly absent after the
training day, and differences between the novice and expert groups were small.
Furthermore, differences between good and poor composers were larger than
differences between composition methods. All of this can be said even more
strongly in the case of speaking, because participants received no training and
had no practice whatsoever at noninteractive speaking. From a performance
standpoint, *composition,* acquired with great difficulty over years and ordinarily
expressed in writing, appears to be the fundamental skill. Method of composition
(dictating, writing on a napkin on an airplane, etc.) is more properly interpreted
as a component of this skill, related to changes in the task environment. However, individual authors may strongly prefer or dislike one method or task environment, as shown above by their ratings of their own compositions, and from
anecdotes known to each of us.

Generalization Issues. Is one-page letter writing, as we have studied, typical of most composing? Yes—for nonprofessional authors. First, writing is by far the most used method of composing. Second, letter writing is probably the type of writing done by most people. Rakauskas (1978) asked some university composition students what type of writing they did outside of classroom assignments. Of 38 students who responded, 81% indicated they wrote letters, with a frequency between one per month and several per day. The second most frequent type of writing was personal journals, which were similar to letters. Third, acquaintances in IBM's Office Products Division have told me that the median length of letters in American business is one page. Visitors to our laboratory from business and education, upon seeing the content and general characteristics of our letter assignments, point out their typicality.

Limitations of Results

Our results are based upon one-page letters composed in an uninterrupted environment by people who are in the upper 20% of the population in intelligence. In addition, although the letters were similar to those that these participants often compose, they were not exactly the same. Unlike in the everyday world, participants did not have discretion about when they would compose them or a chance to think about them in advance, and no time was spent "getting ready," e.g., deciding to compose and getting the required information, pencils, dictation supplies, and paper. The time analysis of subprocesses assumes that these processes do not overlap. Even if this were true, the grain of the analysis to capture correctly the time of each process is critical. Thus, the means should be viewed only as estimates.

SOME THEORETICAL THOUGHTS
ABOUT COMPOSITION

Models of Composition

Unacceptable Models. When one considers alternative psychological models of composition, fixed-order stage models seem to be the straw men (e.g., Flower & Hayes, 1977, and Chapter 2, this volume; Gould, 1978c), regardless of whether they reflect the information-processing influence in experimental psychology or the how-to-write-better literature. Processes, e.g., planning or generating, are interactive rather than independent (Gould, 1978c, 1979). Further, during composition people do not follow a fixed sequence of processes, but alternate back and forth among generating, planning, reviewing, editing, and accessing other information (Gould, 1978a; Flower & Hayes, Chapter 2). (Alternation is not inconsistent with all possible stage models, however.)

One Possible Model.   The gross descriptive model we suggested a few years ago for composing consisted of four processes: generating, planning, reviewing, and accessing other information (Fig. 5.2). Our model is more of a theoretical framework for investigating composition than a detailed description of what goes on in the head during composition. It makes no prediction about the transitions from one process to another because, in fact, these are quite flexible. In our initial studies we looked at the transition probabilities from one process to another, in part to identify repeatable segments that might be amenable to computer automation. But, at levels of interesting grain size and interesting generality across participants, flexibility and lack of predictability best describe composition. (Even so, as part of an ongoing study we continue to look for repeatable segments when authors compose letters and messages at computer-based text-editing terminals.)

Our model assumes that composition is *multilevel,* e.g., planning occurs when contemplating the topic to be described, when developing a mental outline, when generating paragraphs or sentences guided by this goal-oriented outline, when deciding what information is required, when selecting words for a sentence. At a micro-level, unconscious planning occurs when pronunciation of one phoneme is influenced by a plan to say a subsequent phoneme. At any time authors may vary the ''level'' at which they are consciously ''working,'' i.e., allocating limited mental resources. For example, they may show concern for choice of a particular word, concern for flow of a paragraph, concern for grammar, etc. Composition is *iterative,* e.g., authors may plan, then generate,

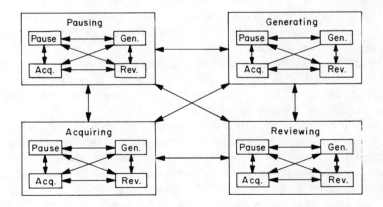

FIG. 5.2   Document creation—a process model.

and, on the basis of feedback, replan and regenerate. Composition can be *recursive,* e.g., a planning function at a high level can "call" itself at a lower level.

An adequate model of composition must allow for overlapping processes. For example, when people first learn to dictate, they do not, at the same time, access information and generate information. With a few hours of practice, however, individuals generally generate (dictate) as they are reading routine (e.g., statistical) facts (Gould, 1978a). An adequate model must allow for learning; e.g., processes that once required attention can become automatic. For example, children must pay attention to letter formation and spelling, but after years of practice these usually do not require conscious attention. Beginning dictators review frequently to make sure the equipment is indeed recording, but after a few hours of practice, this behavior drops out (Gould, 1978a). This automaticity (or elimination of the need for conscious attention) can be complete or partial, and can occur not only at a low level, e.g., letter formation, rapid review, spelling, but also at a much higher level, e.g., knowledge of an audience and of types of composition (letters of recommendation, grant proposals, etc.).

Planning

We have demonstrated quantitatively that planning is the main process in composition, as Flower and Hayes (1977) suggested from protocol data. Planning, on average, was two-thirds of composition time, regardless of composition method, participant's experience with that method, or letter complexity studied so far. But *individual* participants did differ among themselves on this ratio (mean = 65%, range = 48% to 87%, SD = 12% for three experiments in Gould, 1979). Recently when Matsuhashi and Cooper (1978) videotaped four participants who were writing, they found that pause times varied from 47% to 70% of total composition time. Goldman-Eisler (1968), as cited by Bellugi and Fischer (1972), reports participants paused between 40% and 50% of the time when describing picture stories. There are several possible reasons for these somewhat lower values, e.g., precision of measurement, different tasks, exclusion of reading times, precomposing preparation.

One might have assumed that a constant *amount* of planning time would be required regardless of composition method (assuming approximately the same number of ideas or words in each mode). Any difference in the composition time would result from differences in generation time only. This model might be correct if, for example, an author at the outset completely planned a letter and then, afterwards, completely generated it. But the results show that planning time was a constant *proportion* of total composition time. To understand this result, one must realize that planning was local and highly interactive with generating. Authors alternated between brief periods of planning and brief periods of generating. The amount of planning required for each period of generation depended on the method of generation. For example, in comparing writing and speaking, perhaps the necessity to be concerned about spelling, format, graphic appearance, and legibility requires extra time in writing (just as concern about pronunciation and intonation might require extra time in speaking). People may spend more time selecting appropriate words, syntax, and phraseology in writing. Listeners seem more tolerant of false starts and less than optimal grammar and flow than do readers. Prior to actual written output, some authors may first generate in auditory form the words to be written. If this auditory form is not suitable for formal writing, as Flower (1979) has observed in many educated young adults, then time is required to translate it into an appropriate written form. This proportional result could have other interpretations, e.g., planning and generating overlap in some methods (see Gould, 1979).

This means that when total composition time was less for one method than another, as it generally was for speaking versus writing (Gould, 1978c), then planning time was also less. This close association of planning time and generating time raises many interesting questions. Does one process drive the other? If so, which is the driver? Training at planning is presumed to be critical for improved composition (Flower & Hayes, Chapter 2, this volume). But, conversely, would training at generation reduce planning times? It appears that this alternative has been practiced in the elementary and secondary schools in the last decade or two. The emphasis has been upon writing "creatively," even if this means not being restricted by spelling or syntax errors. At best, the results have been mixed (see discussion under Generating).

Flower and Hayes (Chapter 2) have argued that improved composition rests upon improved planning. They describe writing as the "juggling of (mental) constraints." They propose several planning strategies for dealing with this, including temporarily throwing away one constraint, partitioning, satisficing (settling for the first acceptable result, even though it is less than the optimum), and drawing on a well-learned procedure. It should be noted that this analytic planning requires an ability to think ahead, develop clear goals early on, and to think about thinking. This may be possible with some college students and adults. But according to Piaget's theory, such thinking is limited to those who have reached the level of formal operations, which is generally at least high school age. In addition, analytic thinking is not part of the average adult's strategies.

Related to the Flower and Hayes (Chapter 2) suggestion about satisficing is whether authors should use (a) a "spew" strategy, in which they initially create relatively quick, (perhaps) rough first drafts, versus (b) a "first-time final" strategy, in which authors try to make their "first drafts" resemble the eventual final product. Certainly the first might prevent difficulties some writers have, such as backsliding or getting hung up on a detail and losing sight of the main job. An important experiment would be to compare these two strategies for various types of compositions, levels of people, and amounts of time allowed for composing.

The dominance of planning time suggests that conceptual or higher level characteristics are the main limiting factors in composition by people such as we have studied. I assume these conceptual factors relate primarily to the *meaning* of expression, unlike with children whose pause times I assume reflect relatively more difficulties with the *form* of expression. The conceptual factors include formulation and understanding of the problem that triggers the composition and the goals of the composition (see Newell & Simon, 1972, for discussion of goal formulation), experience at composing a particular type of document, knowledge of recipients, including their expectations and knowledge state, an ability to outline and fill in, development of appropriate vocabulary and phrasings, and a secondary working memory not cluttered with irrelevant detail. Although studies of divided attention (see Norman, 1976; Norman & Bobrow, 1975) generally do not consider this latter type of interference, it may be very real. Many famous authors prefer to compose in the morning when their mind is fresh (Paris Review Interviews, 1963). Also, ideas sometimes take "sudden and virtually complete form, as have many of (Roger) Shepard's most original ideas, during a state of hyponopompic suspension before full awakening" (Distinguished Scientific Contribution, 1977). Composition probably has a general component, which is gained through practice in high school, college, and on jobs, and domain-specific components, which are related, for example, to one's professional activity or discipline. As authors develop phrasings, concepts, and points of view, this undoubtedly affects the way they express themselves and, reciprocally, the way they think.

Previous studies have used pauses preceding lexical, syntactic, and semantic units to indicate planning time for utterances (e.g., Goldman-Eisler, 1961; Lindsley, 1975). However, when these studies are examined collectively, this approach is not completely satisfactory (O'Connell, 1977; Rochester, 1973; Rosenberg, 1977). A given pause is not necessarily related exclusively to the next unit (whatever its characteristics). Using total pause time as a measure of planning entire letters, as well as extending pause time analysis to writing, dictating, and typing, is a new approach—without many of the disadvantages of analyzing individual pauses.

In everyday life, planning involves deciding when and where to begin composing. Planning may go on at times when the composer is actually doing other activities, e.g., while waiting for an airplane, shaving, listening to a lecture, driving to work. Lindsay and Norman (1977, Chapter 15) have noted this "unconscious" planning, and they discuss some conditions and factors that influence its occurrence. Matsuhashi and Cooper (1978) allowed for this by giving participants a writing assignment the day before their experiment rather than immediately before they had to compose. An interesting experiment could examine resulting differences of being allowed this additional time to plan.

Generating

Children learn to communicate interactively through talking 5–10 years earlier than they begin to communicate effectively noninteractively through writing. They (and sometimes we) must acquire many subskills that are difficult to learn. Letter formation, neatness, writing in appropriate places on the paper, erasing, formatting, and the rudiments of spelling, punctuation, and word selection take years to master. At first blush one might call these "generation" subskills. But until they are mastered, or become automatic, they require conscious attention, or planning. So one may not want to consider many of them as "generation" subskills until they no longer require conscious planning.

Just how much these attentional demands limit youngsters from more rapidly acquiring higher level aspects of composition is not known. At one extreme, it might not only retard children in school, but prevent them from ever reaching their potential composition levels as adults. However, the pedagogical strategy of de-emphasizing spelling and syntax with the aim of not inhibiting children's creativity in writing may not have attained its goal, as Scardamalia (in press) points out. Indeed, the results sometimes suggest the opposite extreme: that emphasis upon syntax and mechanics of composition are necessary to prevent people from being so hampered by lack of these abilities as to give up on writing. In line with this, Scardamalia (in press) suggests other strategies to meet the desired end without this crippling inadequacy. Shaughnessy (1977) identifies many common errors in composition and recommends exercises to reduce and eliminate them. The claimed success of sentence-combining exercises at improving writing is due, suggest Flower and Hayes (Chapter 2), to making the grammatical or linguistic aspects of sentence generation more automatic, thus freeing attention for other aspects of composition.

What may appear to be higher level generation subskills do not begin to be acquired until after a decade of practice. These include subtle use of words, tone, phraseology, succinctness, good composition practices (e.g., parallel construction, sentence variation, and rhythm), avoidance of bad ones (e.g., run-on sentences, split infinitives, indefinite pronominal references, dangling participles), developing the appropriate context so a wide variety of readers can understand the composition (see Olson's [1977] distinction between utterances and language), a sense of purpose, a sense of audience, figures of speech (e.g., metaphor, simile, alliteration). These, of course, initially require much attention, and for most of us they continue to do so. That indeed is what planning is.

How are different methods of composition related? Flower (1979) believes that, in most cases, writing is speaking to oneself. Only for better writers does composition take on other qualities. If this is correct, then speaking ability sets a limit on writing ability—at least for most people. Scardamalia (in press), after studying 10–14 year old children in academically high achieving classes, feels that spoken (noninteractive) compositions would be of higher quality than the written compositions she received from them. "Writing . . . actually interferes with thought in younger adults," she concludes. Although this seems plausible, my own limited informal observations of children composing indicate that some children make similar errors in speaking and in writing (where this is possible); further, our experiments show high correlations between an adult's ability to compose in writing and speaking. The experiment to test Scardamalia's notion is an important one, and must use an oral composition facility that allows youngsters to generate, edit, and review with the same ease (or difficulty) as they can generate, edit, and review written material. Quality or *maturity* of composition could be assessed by measures that are generally though useful for written composition, e.g., length of T-units—independent clauses with all the attached modifiers (Hunt, 1965, as cited by Matsuhashi & Cooper, 1978; Maimon & Nodine, 1978)—or number of adverbs and adjectives, as well as measures more appropriate for oral composition, e.g., tone or sincerity of the composition, which is greatly affected by intonation and prosody.

That speaking is generally faster than writing (Gould, 1979) could be due not only to differences inherent in the two methods (e.g., potential output rates, required grammar and vocabulary), but also because perhaps people first generate a "spoken" code that must be then translated into a written code.

Writing has developed over the centuries, and now many of its abstract characteristics can be described (e.g., Hecht, 1978). But technology is just now making noninteractive speaking possible (see Gould, 1978b). It remains to be seen whether the characteristics of spoken letters will approximate those of writing or diverge from them. Evidence from the IBM Research Audio Communication System for the last 2 years makes it clear that people can communicate in *noninteractive* speech much more effectively and about much more complicated matters than they initially believe they can. Further, it appears that listeners may be more tolerant of poor flow, false starts, and grammatical errors (in a written sense) than are readers.

Occasionally one encounters the belief that dictation is (potentially) several times faster than writing. This claim is probably based on (1) the fact that one can read aloud about five times faster than one can copy printed material, and (2) the assumption that generation is a major component of total composition time. But our results indicate that dictation is not much faster than writing, at least in part because generation is only about 25% of total composition time. Dictation is not as fast as speaking, and possible reasons for this were suggested previously.

Composition rates are about 13 wpm in writing, 20 wpm in dictating, and 30 wpm in speaking (Gould & Boies, 1978a; Gould, 1978a, 1978c, 1979). Composition rate might be a good measure of composition difficulty, although it has been about the same for all letters we have studied so far. I would assume in real life that composition rates for one's most important personal memos or book chapters might be at least 10 times slower than those found here.

Reviewing

In composing book chapters like this, most of us constantly review our work through many drafts. So do famous literary authors (Paris Review Interviews, 1967). In my experiments, participants spent little or no time reviewing (Gould, 1978c). Initially, I was bothered by this discrepancy. But anecdote and evidence indicate that people in everyday life do not review much. Written personal letters and postcards are perhaps the main type of composition, and these are often not reviewed. Stallard (1974) and Scardamalia (in press) found that high school and university students do not usually revise what they write, and, when required to, find it unpleasant and often a new experience. Emig (1971) pointed out that whereas students do not voluntarily revise school-sponsored writing, they more readily revise self-sponsored writing. As participants learned to dictate in our experiments, they reviewed less and less, apparently gaining confidence in themselves and in the equipment to record faithfully what they had said.

Editing

At the beginning of our experiments on composition, it seemed very possible that a participant would compose deeply and locally. (For example, a three-level example would be: generate a segment and review and change it; review and change the change; and review and change the changed change.) The videotapes consistently showed, however, that participants generally composed at a single level, moving from one segment to another: e.g., plan, generate a phrase or sentence; plan; generate some more; review; change the last segment generated; plan; etc. These results were true for writing, dictating, and speaking. When participants did make changes, they did so "locally" rather than "globally." That is, nearly all changes made were in the last few words composed. This was particularly true for writing, but generally true for dictating and speaking also. Global changes, such as arrows, insertions or deletions of whole sentences, almost never occurred. There was almost no backsliding.

Initially, I was concerned about the typicality of this lack of editing. However, there is evidence that these experimental results may be typical. There are few changes in the handwritten letters we receive (although, while it seems unlikely to me, people who make changes may write the whole letter over). Even college students do not usually revise. Although the information does not bear directly on editing during the first draft, acquaintances in IBM's Office Products Division have told me that the median number of revisions of a letter by authors, once typed by a secretary, is usually zero or one. Indeed, according to Bracewell, Scardamalia, and Bereiter (1978), children must be about 14 or over before they can tailor their writing to various audiences (the authors report, however, that they can adapt their conversations years earlier). Heavy revision may be limited to "professional" writing—as done by professional authors (reporters, essayists, novelists—see Paris Review Interviews, 1967) or people (scientists, engineers, business persons) whose careers are directly affected by how they formulate and communicate their thoughts in writing, oftentimes to large, diverse, and relatively unknown audiences.

Accessing Other Information (Reading, Listening)

Our experiments provide little information on this topic. Participants generally did not make notes or outlines and did not ask to use a dictionary, thesaurus, or reference material. In the tasks where participants had to select some relevant facts from a reference file, they quickly learned to overlap reading and generating.

Computer-Assisted Composition

With computer-based text editors, authors (or their secretaries) can type their compositions into a computer memory. The results are displayed, either on a television-like screen or in hard-copy. Authors can readily insert, delete, move, and modify their text. They can change their composition without typing a whole page over. This limits the area that must be rereviewed. Analogous systems are now possible for noncoded information and for dictating and speaking. Computer-based spelling checkers using large dictionaries and/or algorithms can now automatically verify spelling accuracy, adapt to author input, and suggest correct spelling (e.g., Greanias & Rosenbaum, 1978; Morris & Cherry, 1975). Automatic grammar verification in limited ways also seems possible soon. Computer-based dictating and speaking systems can allow authors to review what they have said, even in sped-up speech, thus reducing the time to review.

We are presently studying authors composing with these systems and comparing the results with results described here.

Computer-based systems offer potential for quickly accessing a variety of information useful while composing, e.g., required facts like personal addresses or reference citations, synonyms, opinions, relevant data. The usefulness of some of these relates to the general issue of strategies in composing. For example, should one risk a "diversion" while composing, or keep at it, filling in later?

Computer text creation systems can generate so-called "personalized form letters." One can imagine a variety of scenarios in which these could be triggered by a few simple commands from an "author" that could potentially control the deferential, informational, requestive, and emotional characteristics of the letter. Presumably this approach would be more efficient. Although most form letters I receive are not effective in eliciting from me the behavior the sender desired, insightful human factors experiments could identify required improvements. An important question is whether computer-composed letters can be so similar to traditionally compose letters that recipients cannot distinguish between them reliably. (Presumably this is a desirable goal, as it does not seem possible to me that artificial intelligence will produce *more* effective letters.)

Attitudes

People's's attitudes toward composition are affected by many factors, including method of composition. Novice dictators did not like to dictate and found it stressful. In contrast, we have observed little hesitancy to compose spoken letters, either in our experiments or by people using the IBM Research Audio Communication System in the course of their daily work. Psychological effort may not always be evident from time and quality measurements of performance, however, and it is important in the future to measure such effort.

Differences Between Experts and Others

What distinguishes successful authors from the rest of us? Are the differences between them and us as large, say, as the differences between master and amateur chess players, major league and amateur pitchers, Nobel prize winning physicists and grade school science teachers? Although there is no quantitative evidence on this question, a person lacking education and composing experience might believe there are huge differences.

Are there "types" of expert composers, e.g., the newspaper reporter, novelist, radio commentator, poet, comedy writer? Our view of composition assumes that an author has some general composition skills and some domain-specific ones. Our results suggest, furthermore, that good authors are good authors, and poor authors are poor authors, regardless of method of composition. Composition is the basic skill and method is secondary. Specific domain skills may be developed over years, but we assume there is positive transfer from one domain to another.

What can be learned from famous authors? There are some commonalities and some differences in the way they work. A main feature that Norman (1976, Chapter 9) finds in his survey of experts in various fields is their emphasis upon practice. This is true of famous literary authors also, as shown in the Paris Review Interviews (1963, 1967), which are collections of chapter-length interviews of famous literary authors. But these authors do not practice at writing in the sense of rehearsals or exercise routines. Rather, they simply practice the art of writing by regularly writing subject matter. According to Paris Review Interviews (1963), Laurence Durrell has been "madly scribbling since the age of eight [p. 2]."

A second commonality is a lifelong and almost daily preoccupation with writing. Most famous writers, claims Paris Review Interviews (1963), "had wished from the first to be writers [p. 2]." Authors discuss their art with other authors. They continually think about their own projects, and "unconscious processing" seems to occur. The French writer Cendrars, for whom writing usually came hard, provides an example of this (Paris Review Interviews, 1967). He recalls one incident in New York: "I went to bed. I went immediately to sleep. I woke up with a start. I began to write, to write. I went back to sleep. I woke up a second time with a start. I wrote until dawn and I went back to bed and back to sleep for good. I woke up at five o'clock that evening. I reread the thing. I had written *Les Paques a New-York* [pp. 42–43]." (Perhaps the lesson here is to keep notepads and pencils available everywhere to take advantage when inspiration arises.)

Third, even for famous writers writing can often be a struggle. There are few Mickey Spillanes or Isaac Asimovs who can turn out several books a year. James Jones said (Paris Review Interviews, 1967), "you have to really work at it to write [p. 238]." Some authors find it extraordinarily difficult to write, e.g., Cendrars. Others go through periods when it is relatively easy to write and periods when it is relatively difficult to write, e.g., the playwright Pinter. In the difficult state, Pinter said (Paris Review Interviews), "I want to write a play, it buzzes all the time in me, and I can't put pen to paper [p. 367]."

Fourth, most well-known authors report that they do much revising, and actual manuscripts show this (Paris Review Interviews, 1967).

Fifth, the rate at which a given author composes varies from book to book. Pinter was told to write his first play "by next week." He argued that it would take 6 months. But under the pressure, he wrote it in 4 days (Paris Review Interviews, 1967, p. 351).

Sixth, the approach that a given author takes varies from book to book. The same author may sometimes write from a plan, as Norman Mailer reports writing *The Naked and The Dead,* and at other times have no plan, as Mailer reports writing *Barbary Shore* (Paris Review Interviews, 1967, pp. 261–262).

Seventh, most writers prefer to discuss their subjects rather than their form. They show a great exactness of thought and speech in doing this, according to the Paris Review Interviews. Hemingway said that it is "bad for a writer to talk about how he writes [Paris Review Interviews, 1963, p. 3]." He feels that ideas on writing should remain unexpressed. Ezra Pound says, "The *what* is so much more important than *how* [Paris Review Interviews, 1963, p. 3]." Saul Bellow rules out discussion of his personal writing habits altogether, indicating, "For the artist to give such loving detail to his shoelaces is dangerous [Paris Review Interviews, 1967, p. 178]." "I never think about form at all, says Katherine Anne Porter [Paris Review Interviews, 1963, p. 3]." "It's bad to think . . . a writer shouldn't think too much, states Henry Miller [Paris Review Interviews, 1963, p. 3]."

Eighth, some literary authors compose with a typewriter, e.g., Albee, and others compose in longhand. Mailer has used both indicating that "as soon as I found myself blocked on the typewriter I'd shift to longhand [Paris Review Interviews, 1967, p. 259]." I have not found a famous writer who dictates.

Ninth, what is the key *fundamental* development in getting a book or play off the ground? Some authors report that it is *ideas,* others say it is *words,* others say it is *character formation,* and others say it is *plot development.*

Tenth, the degree to which authors rely on *plans* (really "pre-plans") differs, as Emig (1971) found in a survey of writers in various fields. Albee reports, "I usually think about a play anywhere from six months to a year and a half before I sit down to write it [Paris Review Interviews, 1967, p. 342]." Norman Mailer kept a detailed file of notes on each character for *The Naked and the Dead,* but had not even a plan for *Barbary Shore.* With it, he said, "I literally never knew where the next day's work was coming from, [Paris Review Interviews, 1967, p. 262]." This does not simply indicate an evolution of expertise at writing, because there does not seem to be a monotonic relation between authors' experience and ease of writing. For several books Cendrars would prepare a list of words in advance (3,000 words for one book), and then use them all. Upon first learning to compose, one is probably more resource limited than data limited (see Norman & Bobrow, 1975), but as sophistication at composition increases, one probably becomes increasingly data limited.

Eleventh, some authors rely on environmental idiosyncrasies when they write. Cendrars describes the necessity for himself and other well-known French writers to write in small enclosed spaces, rather than in large rooms with panoramic views. On the other hand, Mailer prefers a long room with a view. Robert Frost said, "I never write except with a writing board. I've never had a table in my life. And I use all sorts of things. Write on the sole of my shoe [Paris Review Interviews, 1963, p. 11]." Stein (1974, pp. 20–21) has collected the following examples from other investigators. Zola avoided daylight and pulled the shades at midday. Kipling wrote only with the blackest ink he could find. Ben Jonson believed he wrote best while drinking a lot of tea and while stimulated by the purring of a cat and the strong odor of orange peel. Schiller kept rotten apples in his desk. Shelley and Rousseau remained bareheaded in the sunshine. Milton and Descartes lay stretched out. Thoreau built his hermitage. Proust worked in a cork-lined room. Balzac wore a monkish working garb. Schiller immersed his feet in ice-cold water. On the other hand, James Jones said, "I find it easy enough to work anywhere . . . if I don't get *too* drunk every night [Paris Review Interviews, 1967, p. 237]."

Twelfth, unlike the stereotype that famous authors compose late at night in dim garrets, Paris Review Interviews (1963, p. 4) indicate that many often compose in the morning. Perhaps this is because one's working memory is free from interfering detail at this time of day.

Most of these data come from one source—The Paris Review Interviews. However, Emig (1971) warns that interviews with established authors focus on their feelings about writing, rather than on the act of writing itself. After reviewing (1) accounts of writing by and about established writers, (2) dialogues between writers and attuned respondents, (3) analyses by others of evolutions of certain pieces of writing, (4) rhetoric and composition texts and handbooks, and (5) theories of the creative process, Emig concludes that only a limited amount can be learned about the writing process from these sources. She recommends empirical case studies of individual students.

Organizational Principles

Until completing school, people write mainly letters, tests, class assigned essays, and term papers. One organizing principle frequently used in these compositions is a list of loosely related items. A second organizing principle is to write about events chronologically, as Flower (1979) has observed in some technical writers.

Besides lists and temporal sequence, spatial sequence is a third simplifying organizational principle in composition. For example, I have asked participants to write down the names of people who have offices on their aisle. Inevitably, they start from the beginning of their aisle and continue writing until reaching the name of the person at the end of their aisle. When I ask them (or other participants) to write the names of people on their aisle in *alphabetical order,* this is a much harder task. Indeed, frequently they will first make some notes using a spatial organization and then rewrite the names alphabetically. As another example, when asked to count the windows in one's house, one ordinarily proceeds mentally around the outside walls of the house or from room to room. But variations in the requirements of this game, e.g., requiring that one write them in order of size or by color of curtains, makes it much more difficult.

As organizing principles, these three reduce memory burden while composing and do not require reorganization and analytical thinking. But much serious composition does require analytical thinking and new organization of knowledge. This is not easy for many reasons, as Flower and Hayes (Chapter 2, this volume) point out.

Thought and Language

How does one translate thoughts into words in writing, in dictating, or in speaking? Are the processes the same for different generation methods? The relationship between thought and language is debatable, in part because it is difficult to define these two. "According to one view, language is necessary for thought, and determines it; according to the opposite view, the development of thought is prior to, and necessary for, the development of language," writes Cohen (1977, p. 72) in a review of language and thought. "A more intermediate position, adopted by Vygotsky, is that thought and language originate independently in the young child and combine in an interactive relationship at a later state of development." What theorists here call "language" is interactive speech communication. Olson (1977), in describing historical differences between oral interactive conversation and composition (he discussed writing here, but noninteractive speaking or dictating could be similarly described), especially emphasizes that interactive two-person communication has an intrinsic shared-knowledge context about which noninteractive communication must be explicit. However, some noninteractive communication has much shared knowledge, e.g., personal letters. Ability to communicate nonteractively does not develop until about 10 years after ability to communicate interactively.

In composing a particular utterance or sentence, choice of semantics, syntax, and lexical items may not be limited to the fixed hierarchical order as is often suggested, but may all proceed together. Consistent with this are the results by Marslen-Wilson (1975), who showed that people, when quickly repeating what another person is saying (i.e., when shadowing that person), make errors that suggest all three processes interact, rather than proceed serially.

The writing and speaking of congenitally blind people and congenitally deaf people show that experience at *listening* (which precedes and is usually necessary for producing acceptable speech) is almost always essential for satisfactory composition. Deaf people have great difficulty speaking (interactively or noninteractively), whereas blind people's speech is not nearly that limited. Furthermore, the writing of deaf people is generally very poorly developed, even with years of practice, whereas the "writing" (in braille) of blind people may be relatively better developed. Deaf people make errors in composition that are rarely or never made by hearing people. Lenneberg (1967), as cited in *Psychology Today* (1972), provides this example from a deaf student with 11 years of language instruction:

> When his father went shopping, he had nothing to do except to eat something. He remembered his father told him promised to his father not to eat somethings. Later he had a big idea. He went to library room. He walked over his father's new sofa. The sofa was dirty. He opened the box of cigar. He picked one. And he think and remember his father his father told him to do. He putted back it. He leave library room. And one of tiny devil told him disobey his father. "Okay!" He went to back to the library room. He got it. He lighted it. He smoked for one hour. He slept and felt very sick. His father called him. But he did not called. His father thought he ran away [p. 127].

Are these departures from normal English syntax to be considered errors of unaccountable cause, or do they reflect the constructs of a sign language? Bellugi, Klima, and Siple (1975) have concluded that, at the level of short-term memory, the prelingually deafs' language organization reflects the concepts of sign language much more than the concepts of spoken or written language.

Is the limitation of poor writers in their *thinking* or in their *writing*? For example, can they *say* this compositions better than they can *write* them? Scardamalia (in press) believes this. Also, Flower and Hayes (Chapter 2, this volume) write of a bright college student: "She has probably never had to talk much less write about her subject before . . . ." On the other hand, our result that good authors are good authors regardless of method suggests that the limitation is not in a particular method of composition, but rather something more central (thinking?). Of course, this result is based upon college graduates, who presumably are generally above average writers. The probable answer is that the writing of poor writers can be improved through specific writing training, as well as through a general increase in cognitive abilities.

Knowing versus Writing

"How do I know what I think" wrote the well-known author E. M. Forster, "until I see what I say? [quoted in Shaughnessy, 1977, p. 79]." It is often said, especially among English composition teachers, that one does not really know something unless it can be expressed in writing. This was generally accepted, it seemed to me, in discussion at the Carnegie-Mellon Symposium on Composition. But certainly there are examples where this is not true. Illiterates probably "know" they are hungry, cold, aroused, thirsty, angry, in just as certain terms as do the literate. People want others to be nice to them, even if, as they say, they are unable to express it verbally. Writing it down does not necessarily make the desire any more acute or understandable. There are simply things we "know" that we cannot adequately describe verbally. This is what makes for poets, because only a few can capture in writing the thrill of romance, of springtime, of passing an important exam, of a sexual encounter, of watching a baby, of learning that the tumor is benign, of first touring the American West or seeing Big Sur. Although writing (or speaking) often helps clarify one's thinking about some analytic problems, there is much of what we know and feel that, as people say, "I just can't describe." Theories of consciousness, e.g., Ornstein's (1972), support this view.

Taxonomies of Documents

Taxonomies of documents have been developed for purposes of teaching composition and rhetoric, e.g., letters of persuasion, description, etc. Students develop their own taxonomies, e.g., how many words must I write? To be most useful psychologically, a taxonomy must consider not only the type of document but also the skill level of the composer. As Scardamalia (in press) points out, "the complexity of writing tasks is to a large extent defined by the writer." Thus developing a useful psychological taxonomy may be impossible.

Verbal Protocols

Other methodologies for experimental studies of production tasks in general and composition in particular are beginning to develop. Participants have been asked to talk about what they are thinking or what they are writing while they are actually writing, as well as before and after writing (Emig, 1971; Hayes & Flower, Chapter 1, this volume). Initial protocol results make writing appear more complex than do analyses of actual performance results obtained, i.e., the written record or videotapes of composition. Which one is more accurate? It is intuitive that composition is complex (certainly teachers of slow learners can verify this), but some cautions must be raised in interpreting protocol results. Do protocols make automatic processes appear less so? In protocols, are decision points mentioned by participants that, if they did not have to think aloud, would hardly be conscious decisions at all? In the process of providing a verbal protocol, do participants think more analytically than usual, and does this affect the actual composition in unknown ways? What if a "protocol" was obtained afterward, in the sense of a participant viewing his or her performance on videotape, and then commenting upon it, as Matsuhashi and Cooper (1978) propose? Many people find composing difficult, let alone providing a rich, simultaneous commentary while doing it. Indeed, I suspect psychologists who study the interfering effect of one task upon another (e.g., counting backward while remembering a few characters or words) would predict this type of divided attention to have profound interfering effects. Most important, much selection typically occurs before one finds a participant who gives a "good" protocol (Hayes & Flower, Chapter 1). By definition, this selection raises concern about the generality of results. Most adults, and certainly most children, do not think in the analytic, frank, confident, introspective terms required for giving protocols. And most people do not compose in this organized, analytic fashion anyway (Flower, 1979). Nevertheless, the motivation is to identify and understand mental processes in composition—and investigators using protocol analysis are contributing to this difficult goal.

ACKNOWLEDGMENTS

I thank Stephen Boies, John Richards, and John Thomas for their comments on a version of this chapter.

REFERENCES

Bartlett, F. *Thinking: An experimental and social study.* New York: Basic Books, 1958.

Bellugi, U., & Fischer, S. A comparison of sign language and spoken language: Rate and grammatical mechanisms. *Cognition,* 1972, *1,* 173–200.

Bellugi, U., Klima, E. S., & Siple, P. Remembering in signs. *Cognition: International Journal of Cognitive Psychology,* 1974–1975, *3*(2), 93–125.

Boies, S. J., & Gould, J. D. User performance in an interactive computer system. *Proceedings of 1970 Princeton Conference on Information Sciences and Systems,* p. 122. (Abstract)

Boies, S. J., & Gould, J. D. Syntactic errors in computer programming. *Human Factors,* 1974, *16*(3), 253–257.

Bracewell, R. J., Scardamalia, M., & Bereiter, C. *The development of audience awareness in writing.* Unpublished manuscript from talk given at the American Educational Research Association Meeting, Toronto, 1978.

Card, S., Moran, T., & Newell, A. *The manuscript editing task: A routine cognitive skill* (Report No. SSL 76-8). Palo Alto, Calif.: Xerox Palo Alto Research Center, 1976.

Clark, H. The language-as-fixed-effect fallacy: A critique of language statistics in psychological research. *Journal of Verbal Learning and Verbal Behavior,* 1973, *12,* 335-359.

Cohen, G. *The psychology of cognition.* New York: Academic Press, 1977.

Distinguished Scientific Contribution Awards for 1976. *American Psychologist,* 1977, *32,* 54-67.

Emig, J. *The composing processes of twelfth graders* (Research Monograph No. 13). Urbana, Ill.: National Council of Teachers of English, 1971.

Flower, L. Writer-based prose: A cognitive basis for problems in writing. *College English,* 1979, *41,* 19-37.

Flower, L. S., & Hayes, J. R. Problem-solving strategies and the writing process. *College English,* 1977, *39,* 449-461.

Goldman-Eisler, F. Hesitation and information in speech. In C. Cherry (Ed.), *Information theory.* London: Butterworth, 1961.

Gouldman-Eisler, F. *Spontaneous speech.* London: Academic Press, 1968.

Gould, J. D. An experimental study of writing, dictating, and speaking. In J. Requin (Ed.), *Attention and performance VII.* Hillsdale, N.J.: Lawrence Erlbaum Associates, 1978, 299-319. (a)

Gould, J. D. Experiments on document composition. In E. J. Baise & J. M. Miller (Eds.), *Proceedings of 22nd Annual Meeting of Human Factors Society,* 1978, 1-4. (b)

Gould, J. D. How experts dictate. *Journal of Experimental Psychology: Human Perception and Performance,* 1978, *4*(4), 648-661. (c)

Gould, J. D. *Writing and speaking letters and messages.* IBM Research Report, RC-7528, 1979.

Gould, J. D., & Ascher, R. N. *Use of an IQF-like query language by nonprogrammers.* IBM Research Report, RC-5279, 1975.

Gould, J. D., & Boies, S. J. How authors think about their writing, dictating, and speaking. *Human Factors,* 1978, *20,* 494-505. (a)

Gould, J. D., & Boies, S. J. Writing, dictating, and speaking letters. *Science,* 1978, *201,* 1145-1147. (b)

Gould, J. D., & Drongowski, P. An exploratory study of computer program debugging. *Human Factors,* 1974, *16,* 258-276.

Gould, J. D., Lewis, C., & Becker, C. A. *Writing and following procedural, descriptive, and restrictive syntax language instructions.* IBM Research Report, RC-5943, 1976.

Gould, J. D., & Quinones, A. Handwriting and speech signal analyzer. *IBM Technical Disclosure Bulletin,* 1978.

Greanias, E. G., & Rosenbaum, W. S. Automatic spelling verification: Towards a system solution for the office. *IBM Technical Directions,* 1978, *4*(4), 17-23.

Hecht, P. *The relational dialectic in mediated communications.* Unpublished manuscript, University of Colorado, 1978.

LaBerge, D., & Samuels, S. J. Toward a theory of automatic information processing in reading. *Cognitive Psychology,* 1974, *6,* 293-333.

Lenneberg, E. *The biological foundation of language.* New York: Wiley, 1967.

Lindsay, P. H., & Norman, D. A. *Human information processing.* New York: Academic Press, 1977.

Lindsley, J. R. Producing simple utterances. How far ahead do we plan? *Cognitive Psychology,* 1975, *7,* 1-19.

Maimon, E. P., & Nodine, B. F. Measuring syntactic growth: Errors and expectations in sentence-combining practice with college freshmen. *Research in Teaching English,* 1978, *12*(3), 233-244.

Marslen-Wilson, W. D. Sentence perception as an interactive parallel process. *Science,* 1975, *189,* 226–228.

Matsuhashi, A., & Cooper, C. *A video time-monitored observational study: The transcribing behavior and composing processes of a competent high school writer.* Unpublished manuscript from talk presented at the American Educational Research Association Meeting, Toronto, 1978.

Miller, G., & Johnson-Laird, P. *Language and perception.* Cambridge, Mass.: Harvard University Press, 1976.

Morris, R., & Cherry, L. L. Computer detection of typographical errors. *IEEE Trans on Professional Communication,* 1975, *18*(1), 54–64.

Newell, A., & Simon, H. A. *Human problem solving.* Englewood Cliffs, N.J.: Prentice-Hall, 1972.

Norman, D. A. *Memory and attention* (2nd ed.). New York: Wiley, 1976.

Norman, D. A., & Bobrow, D. G. On data-limited and resource-limited processes. *Cognitive Psychology,* 1975, *7,* 44–64.

O'Connell, D. C. One of many units: The sentence. In S. Rosenberg (Ed.), *Sentence Production.* New York: Wiley, 1977.

Olson, D. R. From utterance to text: The bias of language in speech and writing. *Harvard Educational Review,* 1977, *47*(3), 257–282.

Ornstein, R. E. *The psychology of consciousness.* San Francisco: Freeman and Company, 1972.

Paris Review Interviews. *Writers at Work.* Second Series. New York: Viking Press, 1963.

Paris Review Interviews. *Writers at Work.* Third Series. New York: Viking Press, 1967.

Psychology Today—An Introduction. Del Mar, Calif.: CRM Books (2nd Ed.), 1972.

Rakauskas, W. Some student views on writing. *Pennsylvania Council of Teachers of English Bulletin,* 1978, *37,* 21–26.

Rochester, S. R. The significance of pauses in spontaneous speech. *Journal of Psycholinguistic Research,* 1973, *2,* 51–81.

Rosenberg, S. Semantic constraints on sentence production: An experimental approach. In S. Rosenberg (Ed.), *Sentence Production.* New York: Wiley, 1977.

Scardamalia, M. How children cope with the cognitive demands of writing. In C. H. Frederiksen, M. F. Whiteman, & J. F. Dominic (Eds.), *Writing: The nature, development and teaching of written communication.* Hillsdale, N.J.: Lawrence Erlbaum Associates, in press.

Shaughnessy, M. P. *Errors and expectations.* New York: Oxford University Press, 1977.

Stallard, C. K. An analysis of the writing behavior of good student writers. *Research in Teaching of English,* 1974, *8,* 206–218.

Stein, M. I. *Stimulating creativity: Vol. 1. Individual procedures.* New York: Academic Press, 1974.

Thomas, J. C., & Gould, J. D. A psychological study of query-by-example. *Proceedings of 1975 National Computer Conference,* 1975, 439–445.

6 Specific Thoughts on the Writing Process

P. C. Wason
University College London

Four fairly interesting things can be said about the psychological processes involved in writing: (1) some highly articulate individuals are conspicuously incapable of writing at all; (2) procrastination is the one prevailing symptom that tends to affect us all; (3) there is a mild taboo surrounding the topic that cannot altogether be explained by invoking rational reasons of esteem or competition; and (4) those who do enjoy writing do so in large measure because it helps them to think.

I intend to discuss some of these things, but I do not attempt to offer you a definitive program, or even a finished canvas. Rather let me try to give you a few small insights based on my personal experience as a writer and a teacher. I want to start with some little things—symptoms of a more general malaise: the kinds of sentences that crop up in Ph.D. theses, papers submitted for publication, or even grant applications. For many years now I have kept a personal file on them. Here are three:

1. Although using names which actually included the attribute values to be detected might, at the learning stage, have given a clue about the structure of the universe of concepts to subjects who in theory had no knowledge of this, the use of an unsystematic set of names would have ruled out a method of learning names, by learning the rules for forming names, which it was originally thought would be used for one of the experimental groups.

2. Subjects knew that of the specified four values of three dimensions, three values were included and one was not, with positive instances, if three values of one dimension were present, then these were included or were correct; if one value was absent, ipso facto, the other three values were part of the concept.

Conversely, if four values of a dimension were present, that dimension was irrelevant. With negative instances, a repeated value was incorrect or excluded, and the other values in that dimension were included. To identify the incorrect value of a dimension, was to have information which could lead to identification of values of the other relevant dimension, which the incorrect value nullified.

3. If there are accumulated store totals attributes corresponding to stores in which there are store totals are preferred in order of size of store total and thereafter (and in the case of ties between store totals) at random.

This last one, significantly enough, was not from the first draft of a thesis, but from a submitted grant proposal. Obviously something had gone wrong with the typing, but did the author read it through? In such sentences, each written by a different person, there are at least four possible reasons for confusion:

1. The writers are unaware that their words could cause any difficulties.
2. The writers suppose that they could express themselves in no simpler way because of the supposed complexity of the subject matter.
3. The writers think that the reader should make a supreme effort to follow the profundity of their thought.
4. They simply couldn't care at all.

In supervising Ph.D. students I have diagnosed each of these reasons. However, often a remarkable thing happens when I put my finger on monstrous sentences and ask students to read them aloud. They immediately say, "What I was trying to say was such-and-such." I am always tempted to reply, "Then why didn't you say it?" The words they utter turn out to be more direct and unaffected than the words they wrote. But the question would have been wrong. I do not think the difference lies between writing and speaking. I think that students' interpretations of their own writing, spoken in response to my objection, were not apparent to them when the original sentences had been written. It was not that they had had a clear thought, but failed to find the right words in which to express it. The thought had not at the time been discovered. And it had not had time to be discovered because of the writer's low criterion for "prose acceptability." Insufficient efforts had been made to put a sentence in another way, let alone in a simpler way. I return to this topic when I consider my own hypothesis about writing.

But now I want you to consider the official prose of government departments. We found that many nonstatutory leaflets, intended to explain Social Security to the man in the street, were largely incomprehensible to psychology postgraduates. Here are two passages from them:

A Class I contribution is not payable for employment by any one employer for not more than 8 hours in any week—but if you normally work for more than 8 hours in any week for any one employer, a Class I contribution is payable except for any week when you do not do more than 4 hours work for that employer.

Contributions paid late cannot normally count for death grant (other than towards the test of yearly average) unless they were paid before the death on which the grant is claimed and before the death of the insured person if that was earlier. But if the insured person died before the person on whose death the grant is claimed, contributions which, although paid late, have already been taken into account for the purpose of a claim for widow's benefit or retirement pension, will count towards death grant. [One begins to wonder *who* has died.]

It might be argued that such language betrays a contempt for the reader. But I do not wish to argue that. A simpler assumption is that the logical relations between interconnected rules are just too complex to express in prose. Sheila Jones and I (Jones, 1968) have demonstrated that it is more rational to reduce such material to a series of "atomic propositions," like a computer program, so that the individual case, acting like a computer, automatically selects only those propositions that are relevant. The Treasury smiled benevolently, but our enthusiasm for the cause was not fired by a casual remark of the Minister (Dick Crossman): "Too much clarity has its dangers."

In general, instructions provide a rich field for the potential writer because they may (dramatically) test the appropriateness of each word. It has been alleged that the cause of a plane crash was due to one word in the maintenance manual. At the subsequent inquiry the engineer was asked what the manual said. "Remove the pin, examine it, and if it is bent replace it." He was then asked what he did. "I removed the pin, saw it was bent and replaced it [pushed it in again]." Similarly, the officials responsible for designing a "10% census" form consulted me about the questions because a pilot study had revealed some curious answers. One question went like this: "If you were born in one of the counties, state the exact address; if born in London, state locality." Some answers consisted of one word: "locality." Surely we would not have been surprised if a computer had done likewise. In both cases I have cited, the careless use of one word had unexpected consequences. Such sins, which only become startling in imperative or interrogative contexts, are merely symptoms of an inability, or unwillingness, to *test* our words against the hypothetical understanding of a potential audience.

I think I learned this the hard way. In 1946 I started weekly tutorials with Lord David Cecil at Oxford. My first essay was on the "Faerie Queene." With hands trembling on the paper I started to read it aloud. In the middle Cecil could sit still no longer and jumped up and drew the heavy curtains along their brass rings. Surviving this new trauma, I struggled on to the end. "That's all right as far as it goes, but what exactly do you mean by the *delicacy* of Spenser's poetry?" What on earth did I mean? For the first time I really appreciated that I must be absolutely clear about what my words were intended to mean, that I should draw out my thought rather than resort to vague labels.

When I became a psychologist I developed a routine for writing papers about my research. And from this routine I developed a hypothesis about writing (Wason, 1970). The hypothesis is that writing is difficult for some people because they try to do two incompatible things at the same time: say something, and say it in the most acceptable way. When I feel ready to write, I put a pad of blank paper on my desk and write down my thoughts, guided by the notes or raw data relevant to my task, using a pen with a broad nib which at least carries the illusion that my words have some weight. These rituals are doubless superstitious, but two rules are more rationally motivated: (1) the complete paper, or chapter, must as far as possible be written at a single session; and (2) no sentence is reread or altered. Thus I suppose I belong to "configuration 4" in Hayes and Flower's scheme (Fig. 1.12).

This first phase is creative, but it usually feels extremely painful and uninspired because little is elaborated or connected. It is important neither to allow my critical faculties to be alerted, nor to abandon the task in disgust at my own indifferent performance. The aim is simply to exteriorize thought without regard to its expression and in accordance with the cliché that you don't know what you are trying to say until you have said it. It finds an echo in what Freud said to Joan Riviere (1958): "Write it, write it, put it down in black and white . . . get it out, produce it, make something of it—outside you: give it an existence independently of you [p. 49]." This initial phase entails that no sequential organization be imposed other than the one that occurs spontaneously. If the thoughts do not come to fill out a point, I do not ruminate but go on to another point. This is like sculpting, or composing (or solving) a chess problem in which attention is not restricted to the function of particular pieces (analogous to specific words). In writing it frees my attention from the bonds of serial order, from the struggle with linearity. The heuristics used in this phase, with their strong emphasis on play, have been extremely well documented by Flower and Hayes (1977).

The intention of the second phase is critical. The text is reordered, sentences are changed, and a lot is simply deleted. Usually I write between the lines in a different colored ink, and code paragraphs with symbols that refer to a more appropriate order. This process may be continued over several days, and after repeated rereadings. The assembly of the text becomes less like composing a chess problem, in which insight is important, and more like the completion of a jigsaw puzzle, in which units have a definite shape. My most characteristic reaction is: "How on earth could I have said that? What I was obviously trying to say was such-and-such." But was it? It is more likely that I have only now discovered what to say. Isn't this like the student who has written an obscure sentence and then sees what he means when challenged? He had merely stopped too soon; it is in learning when not to stop that progress is made.

The third phase is a complete redraft. In my experience the desire to do this has a compelling force that I do not understand. Perhaps it is only an example of what psychologists call the "Zeigarnik effect," the tendency to recall uncompleted tasks. The second phase aimed merely to structure thought, but in the third phase the cool, detached process of further clarification frequently generates new thought, and I begin to write the whole piece in another way. This interaction may be related to the dialectical relation between thought and language expounded by Vygotsky (1962). The process of criticism becomes creative. It does not merely refashion language, it enlarges thought. Scrutiny of language alters the thought expressed in language. This hypothesis might be tested by getting individuals to generate lists of ideas relevant to a given issue as a function of (a) writing and (b) thinking. If my hypothesis is correct, then writing should be more productive than thinking.

I have some backing for the generality of my procedures, if not for my hypothesis. In 1976 David Lowenthal and I distributed a questionnaire (Lowenthal & Wason, 1977) about the enjoyment of writing to the entire academic staff of University College London. Every attitude—love, hate, and ambivalence between them—characterized the 170 replies (17%) that were returned. But the main finding was that those who planned their writing ahead of time generally disliked the process; those who could think only as they wrote enjoyed it most. Consider these quotes:

A historian: "The process of writing represents a progress towards an exact clarification of thoughts and conclusions for myself."

A mathematician: "Writing is part of the research; in striving to make the work intelligible, results improve and arguments get simpler and more elegant."

Another historian: "One of the cheering things about writing is that it often clears my mind and stimulates ideas and directions of arguments which I had not thought of."

A lawyer: "In doing the groundwork I begin to see a way of solving intellectual problems. . . . Writing is the fruition of these internal dilemmas, struggles, breakthroughs."

Another historian: "For me, literary composition is part of the process of scholarly research and discovery; for only in the course of working out exactly how I wish to present findings in my subject do I finally arrive at the discovery of what I have found out."

One last quote epitomizes these themes:

Writing for me is an experience of knowing what to say. I can make endless schemes of how the piece should run but it never comes out according to plan. Until I have written a paragraph, I do not even know whether what I am saying is true. Once it is down in black and white I frequently see that it is not and then I have to ask myself why it is not.

However, a research student of mine, Estelle Phillips, who is conducting research on how Ph.D. research is done, claims that she has found two cases of opposite ''cognitive styles'' in writing. Both individuals are in the same academic department, and both say they enjoy writing very much. The comment of the ''serialist'' writer is inconsistent with our own findings: ''Writing is like building a wall, and then papering it. I don't see how one can begin to write individual paragraphs before you have a plan of the whole; each paragraph modifies all the others. The important thing is getting the ideas in order. The style is already there in the skeleton.'' The ''wholist'' writer, on the other hand, makes a comment consistent with our findings: ''I write a complete first draft in longhand. As I go along I tend to revise a bit, but when I've finished I revise a great deal and it tends to look like World War III on paper. If I'm really interested in it I'll start at 8:30 or 9:30 a.m. and go on until late at night. Once I start I want to see it finished; the shorter the time between conception and finished article the better.'' Remarks such as these suggest, with their clear distinction between opposite approaches, that we should view our own main finding with caution.

Let me now say a little more about the first draft because I am inclined to think that the Hayes and Flower admirable model of the composition process does not capture the obscure motivational dynamics associated with it. I said at the beginning that the one prevailing symptom associated with writing is procrastination. Why should this be so? I think it is because we tend to regard any serious piece of writing as a ''natural process'' like childbirth or defecation—something which has to be waited for, and which takes over at the right moment. This would, of course, account for the taboo that I also mentioned. The casual and friendly question: ''How is the book (paper, essay, thesis) going?'' is often met with shy looks and evasive replies. It has even been suggested to me (Richard Barrett, personal communication) that writing may be taboo because, like excrement or menses in primitive society, it lies on the boundary between the self and the not-self. Is it still a part of oneself, or does it belong to the objective world of ideas, Popper's ''World Three''?

At any rate something of the peculiar agony of the first draft is described by one of our respondents:

> The initial gurgitation of material builds up high pressure of nervous excitement, leading to such physical symptoms as redness in the face, headache, inability to sit down, lapses of concentration and extreme short temper, especially on interruption. Ordering of the material presents agonizing problems of rethinking and usually destroying whole bodies of the original material; problems of sequence often lead to inability to write down a coherent sentence.... The final process [is] well nigh unendurable!

This sounds like the consequences of ''forced writing.'' The idea of waiting for the right moment was expressed by one of the Ph.D. students (an architect) studied by Estelle Phillips of University College London:

I realize now that writing is a very intuitive process. Writing is like drawing. At one time I thought that drawing could be a mechanical activity. I didn't think it was related in any way to one's mood or state of mind . . . one does have to develop the discipline to be able to get in the right mood often enough . . . that's exactly what's happened to me with writing . . . when I do get in the mood I'm able to sit down and write several sentences without changing a word or a phrase. It's fun, it's really a good experience. There are other times when I try to force myself to write and it's a struggle all the way. It comes out stilted and I can't get the phrasing right and inevitably I end up tossing it all away.

And yet it seems to me that the ''natural process'' theory of writing may be a myth founded on romantic notions of creativity with their emphasis on freedom from external constraints. One way to puncture this myth is to impose strict deadlines on oneself and others; with luck such decisions become internalized as imperatives—at least they always do in my own case. It might be thought that such procedures would lead to ''forced writing'' with all the symptoms that have been described. But this is not inevitable. Writing may be especially difficult when the writer sees the task as unbounded in time. When a goal is set, and an explicit contract is made, the task may be appreciated as finite, and the pain ameliorated. After all, much journalism and technical reporting has to be completed within defined time limits. This, I think, is what the architect student had in mind when he talked about ''the *discipline* to be able to get in the right mood.''

But there is another way that may be just as effective. It is usually assumed that writing is essentially a private activity, but is this assumption justified? In my view we should pay more attention to writing a single text in collaboration with others. In many different spheres we have to collaborate to achieve our ends, and there is no reason why this should not be done in writing. I have written many papers and three books in this way. Joan Williams and I (Wason & Williams, 1978) have found that getting school children to write a story by generating alternate sentences, with the constraint that the final text must seem to have been written by one individual, is a powerful motivational device. It demands, for one thing, that each child should try to ''decenter'' from his own point of view and accommodate to the thought of another. Of course, in expository writing a looser technique has an added bonus: One individual feels obligated to ''take over'' the work when the other gets satiated.

The Open University has institutionalized collaborative writing with great success in the production of texts that must hold the student's interest because such texts are designed for ''teaching at a distance'' and are distributed as correspondence. They are not conventional texts to supplement lectures and face-to-face teaching; they are ''written tutorials.'' As a consultant to the Open University I have learned the benefits of writing such texts. Each of three drafts of a ''course unit'' is constructively criticized by members of the course team and by other consultants. In addition, comments are likely to be received from all over the country by Open University tutors. I have enjoyed considering all these criticisms, which range from the global to the detailed, and modifying my own writing to take account of them. Indeed, at present I am writing about these procedures with a lecturer on the staff of the Open University (Wendy Stainton Rogers), who subjected my own "course unit" to "development testing." And we are doing this collaboratively, too. After a brief planning session we each wrote an independent draft and then met again to see how we could weld what we had written into a single text. This turned out to be a stimulating experience because it became obvious that each of us had "got over" certain points better than the other.

It is worth commenting on the style of Open University "course units." It has to be one that is not only devoid of gratuitous jargon, but that encourages the author to say just why he became interested in doing the research in the first place. According to Ravetz (1971), the constraints exerted upon the scientific paper preclude this because they present the results of research "out of the context of their creation and in a simplified or vulgarized version [p. 104]." But I should like to argue that it is sometimes therapeutic to overcome these constraints because in so doing we may learn more about our own research. A scientific paper is not a list of facts or observations; it contains an argument that seeks to modify existing knowledge. Inferences have to be drawn, and data have to be interpreted, and these activities involve a personal decision to select what is relevant; all that must be "objective" are the operations upon which the observations rest. There is some backing for these remarks in a little-known radio broadcast by Medawar (1964):

> The scientific paper is a fraud in the sense that it does give a totally misleading narrative of the processes of thought that go into the making of scientific discoveries. . . . The discussion which in the traditional paper goes last should surely come at the beginning. The scientific facts and scientific acts should follow the discussion, and scientists should not be ashamed to admit, as many *are* apparently ashamed to admit, that hypotheses appear in the mind along uncharted by-ways of thought; that they are imaginative and inspirational in character; that they are indeed adventures of the mind.

I do not think this provocative declaration is meant to demolish the conventional scientific paper as a source of value to the specialist. It is meant to demolish it as an account of the way in which research is done. There is scope for both kinds of writing. The paper is the scientist's bread and butter, but articles of a less specialized sort—scientific journalism if you like—enable us to keep our hand in, and regain an authentic voice. In addition, the search for clarity and clear exposition will tend to preserve our language from the entropy that always threatens it.

I am all too conscious that I have said next to nothing about the improvement of writing skills, which is the theme of this book. In my experience ''models of style'' and precepts about how writing should be done have had little effect on my students. Two of them, who once wrote very indifferent prose, have developed into first-class writers; others have not been conspicuously successful. One must attack each time the concrete case, a practice that is brought to a fine art in the Oxford undergraduate tutorial. And one must urge students to attack their own concrete cases themselves by testing their own words against an interested but critical hypothetical audience. This might best be achieved by allowing students to take turns in being critics and authors, in the hope that the role of the critic would eventually become internalized. It would at least avoid the authoritarian spirit, which can always creep into the teacher–pupil relationship. There seems to me no substitute for practice, and for the constant question: ''What exactly do I mean by that?''

REFERENCES

Flower, L. S., & Hayes, J. R. Problem-solving strategies and the writing process. *College English,* 1977, *39,* 449–461.

Jones, S. *Design of instruction.* London: Her Majesty's Stationery Office, 1968.

Lowenthal, D., & Wason, P. C. Academics and their writing. *Times Literary Supplement,* June 24, 1977, p. 782.

Medawar, P. B. Is the scientific paper a fraud? In D. Edge (Ed.), *Experiment.* London: B.B.C. publications, 1964.

Ravetz, J. R. *Scientific knowledge and its social problems.* Oxford: Oxford University Press, 1971.

Riviere, J. A character trait of Freud's. In J. D. Sutherland (Ed.), *Psychoanalysis and contemporary thought.* London: Hogarth, 1958.

Vygotsky, L. S. *Thought and language.* Cambridge, Mass.: MIT Press, 1962.

Wason, P. C. On writing scientific papers. *Physics Bulletin,* 1970, *21,* 407–408.

Wason, P. C., & Williams, J. E. Collaborative writing games. *Resources in Education,* 1978, *13*(7).

7 Teaching Writing by Teaching the Process of Discovery: An Interdisciplinary Enterprise

Lee Odell
State University of New York at Albany

Let us begin with a point on which we all agree: There is, in fact, a writing crisis. Many of our students are not accustomed to writing at all; most of them do not write as fluently, as perceptively, or even as correctly as we might wish. Furthermore, the problem is not limited to our own classes; there is no reason to think that our own students have singled us out for special abuse. Our colleagues in other departments—at least those who require students to do very much writing—feel the same frustration we feel when we read students' writing.

Comforting as this shared feeling may be, it is not enough to voice our mutual frustration, proclaim that a crisis really does exist, and return to our classrooms, soothed by the knowledge that we are not alone. Nor will it do to spend our time trying to decide who is to blame for the present state of affairs. It is, of course, an amusing game to see how many ways we can complete the sentence "Students do not write well because . . . ." They do not write well because the freshman composition program at our school is not very good; because high schools offer too many elective courses; because our society is too permissive; because the third edition of Webster's dictionary does not distinguish between standard and nonstandard usage.

Any one of these explanations is about as plausible as any of the others. But all of them miss the point that what has been called a writing crisis is, in fact, a teaching crisis. Students do not write well because they are not taught to write. Indeed, they are frequently taught (by widespread use of multiple choice tests and by superficial comment on the little writing they are asked to do) that writing is not very important at all. If we want students to write better, teachers in every discipline will have to insist that students write. And all of us—not just teachers of composition or teachers of English—will have to teach students to write, or at least help them learn to do the sort of writing required by the particular courses we are offering.

As a composition teacher, I make this latter recommendation with some reluctance. After all, my colleagues in other departments do not expect me to help them teach history or mathematics or economics. I can justify my recommendation only by making two assumptions. The first is that the job of improving students' writing is simply too complex, too time consuming to be undertaken by any one course or any one discipline. My second assumption is that the act of writing can be a means whereby students can master the content of almost any course we offer. (One possible exception might be a course that emphasizes musical or other artistic performance rather than the analysis of music or of the other arts.)

Committed as I am to these assumptions, I must point out that they make sense only if we agree upon what *teaching writing* does and does not include. I hope you will grant me that teaching writing is not simply a matter of correcting spelling, improving syntax, stamping out mistakes in usage. Of course we should be concerned about students' mastery of the conventions of standard written English. But when I propose that all of us teach writing, I am suggesting:

1. that we identify and teach some of the basic processes students will need to use in discovering what they wish to say concerning the topics about which we ask them to write;

2. that we use frequent short writing assignments as a means of engaging students in and helping them examine these processes.

From these two recommendations, it must be clear that I am asking that we think of writing as a process of discovery, a process of exploring, a process of creating, testing, and refining hypotheses. As we teach students how to engage in this process, we increase their chances of learning and performing well in our individual subject areas.

(I use the phrase "increase their chances" advisedly. I know of nothing that will reduce the process of discovery to a neat set of rules that, if followed carefully, will lead inevitably to a valid hypothesis. I suggest only that the process of discovery is not entirely mysterious and that students deserve much more help with this process than they normally receive.)

THE COMPOSING PROCESS:
AN INTROSPECTIVE VIEW

In other articles in this volume, Linda Flower and J. R. Hayes have provided us with one set of terms to characterize what goes on during the process of composing. I should like for us to consider the composing process from a more personal perspective. To arrive at this perspective, would you call to mind an extended piece of writing you have done recently—an article, a paper intended for some scholarly meeting, an exceptionally long letter or memo addressed to colleagues—preferably a piece of writing that required you to do a good deal of careful thinking, perhaps a bit of reading or analyzing data? As you recall that piece of writing, would you consider a series of questions?

1. What was the piece of writing? For whom was it intended?
2. Try to recall one of the first times you actually sat down to write, a time at which you had gathered all the information you needed. How did you begin? Did you dash off several pages? Did you make an outline?
3. What were you thinking about as you began? What thoughts or feelings were you conscious of as you were writing?
4. Were there any points at which you got stuck, just could not think of what you wanted to say next? If there were, how did you get past those stuck points?

If you have begun to remember your own composing process, I invite you to compare it with my answer to the question "What do you do when you write?"[1]

Some time ago, I accepted an invitation to address a state English council meeting on the topic "Teaching and Research in Composition: What Have We Learned during the Past 30 Years?" I had never attended a meeting of the state council before, and my own perspective on teaching and research only goes back to the mid-1960s. Consequently, I went to some pains, gathering perhaps 60 or 70 note cards, each summarizing what seemed to me an important article. Before I began to write, I tried to get some grasp of my subject by identifying major themes running throughout the articles. The ensuing problems were predictable. For one thing, I could think of several quite different ways to categorize the claims made in a given set of articles. Still more troublesome, there would be times when a category would begin to seem clear until I would discover some new note card that would strain my category, forcing me to redefine it or discard it altogether. I persisted in this for a day, trying to invent some stable categories and thereby determine what I wished to say about my assigned topic.

After poring over note cards, looking for some grand insight that would make sense of all my diverse information, I decided to try to begin writing. Because the process was going rather badly, I decided to keep a running commentary on my progress. The first entry on my writing tablet was not part of my presentation, but a note to myself: "Feeling sick at my stomach, really don't want to write. Not sure who'll be in the audience or how they'll react to what I'll say. Not sure right now that I'll seem like much of an expert on this topic." Frequently, writing a note to myself helps me get started. But not this time. So I looked for a quote,

---

[1] I learned the usefulness of asking this question from Robert Gundlach of Northwestern University.

copied it verbatim—just to get myself started putting words on paper—and then tried to explain why I disagreed with it. I started to rant and rave a bit, actually: "This is so offensive and transparent, so simple-minded that it seems hardly worth refuting." I went on in this vein, attacking the intelligence and the motives of the writer. After a while, I read back over my tirade, realized that of course it would not do, and also began to realize that what I was really concerned about was teachers' attitudes toward research. Then I formulated an assertion about these attitudes, and that assertion became one of the main points in my presentation. In retrospect, I can see that my assertion was influenced somewhat by information on the note cards and somewhat by what I had said in attacking the ideas in the passage I had copied. But when I started writing, I had no notion that I wished to make this assertion. I suspect that even if, at the outset, someone had said to me, "Oh, what you really want to say is . . . ." and then quoted my assertion, it would not have registered. I had not discovered it. I had not yet learned it.

I have asked that we consider our own composing processes partly because we need to remind ourselves of the complexity, the uncertainty, the frustration, even the fear that often attends that process. We also need to remind ourselves of the satisfaction that we feel when our ideas begin to come clear, the excitement we experience in finding out exactly what we do think and seeing our ideas take shape on the page. In our concern, sometimes in our despair, about student writing, we have to keep these two points in mind. The first should lead us to examine our teaching practices; it may very well be that we ask students to write under conditions that we ourselves would not find helpful. The second point, the excitement that comes with discovery, should give us some hope, for the very process of learning, which can make writing so difficult and unpleasant, is also our most compelling motivation for writing. I accept Donald Murray's (1978b) claim that "As writers, we are drawn forward to see what argument comes forth in our essays, to find out if hero becomes victim in our novels, to discover the reason for an historic event in our biographies, to experience the image which makes the blurred snapshot in our memory come clear in our poems [1978b, p. 57]." As teachers of writing, whatever our academic discipline, we can take some encouragement in the fact that the process of writing, especially as it entails a process of learning or discovery, can have enough inherent rewards to help us and our students persist despite the uncertainty or unhappiness that also occurs during the composing process. Our problem as teachers is to do what we can to help students negotiate this uncertainty and, again, *increase their chances* of arriving at insights or hypotheses that they will find rewarding. To repeat one of my basic assumptions: Given the complexity of this process, I do not think we can count on any one course or any one discipline to give students all the assistance they need. All of us will have to take some responsibility for teaching students how to write—at least insofar as writing entails a process of learning or discovery.

THE PROCESS OF DISCOVERY

At times, the process of discovery may lead us to make major changes in our understanding of a given topic; we may no longer think or feel as we once did. More frequently, for me at least, the process of discovery entails a revision of existing structures, a heightened sense of a relationship between X and Y, a clearer understanding of the implications of a given assumption. In either case, the process entails: (1) periods of conscious, focused intellectual activity; (2) periods during which a given topic is apparently not foremost in my thoughts; and (3) a point at which a hypothesis occurs, usually an assertion that can be traced only in part to the conscious activity I have been engaged in.

This process of discovery may go on in any number of ways. I consider only three, all of which seem reasonably accessible, all of which seem useful in any discipline. For purposes of analysis, I consider them separately. Later I suggest, for purposes of teaching, ways in which these modes of discovery might be interrelated. My suggestions and my descriptions of the process of discovery are drawn from several sources: current theory, writers' introspective accounts of their composing process, and a distressingly small amount of empirical research.[2]

Writing as Discovery

Some writers, both colleagues and students, have indicated to me that much of the process of discovery takes place before they actually begin to write a draft. But other writers and researchers (e.g., Murray, 1978a, and Elbow, 1975) report that the very act of writing can serve as a means by which one discovers what one wishes to say. Moreover, Janet Emig (1977, p. 122) makes a persuasive argument that some of the attributes of the writing process and written products "correspond to certain powerful learning strategies." I would give especial emphasis to Emig's point that written language offers unique opportunities for analysis and revision of our ideas. Unlike our thoughts or spoken assertions, written assertions have a degree of permanence. With writing, we may come back to our exact phrases (rather than the near approximation that memory sometimes provides) and cross-examine ourselves as rigorously as we can bear: When I make this statement, do I mean X or Y? If I mean X, how can I reconcile that statement with what I have said previously? If I modify X, how does the modification affect what I wish to say later in my argument?

Sometimes the act of writing serves the process of discovery in oblique ways. Some of us write at length only to discover what we do *not* think. And in seeing

---

[2]In the past 15 years, there has been a great deal of research on written composition. But most of these studies have reported on the effectiveness of specific teaching procedures or on the features (especially syntactic features) of written products.

what we do not believe, we begin to get a sense of what we do believe.[3] Or sometimes we may forge ahead with a draft, uncertain of exactly what we want to say but just trying to get words onto paper. On rereading the draft, we find that some of our writing is totally pointless but that some assertions form what Elbow (1975, pp. 35–37) would call a "center of gravity"; that is, we recognize some implicit assumption, some previously unidentified implication in our writing. We make this explicit and, as I did in preparing my paper on research in composition, we try to develop this assertion, finding perhaps that it becomes one of the important points we want to make in the final draft of our writing.

Occasionally, even the process of editing may involve discovery. An apparently small consideration such as transitions may lead us to rethink an entire passage of a paper. Sometimes I will find a sentence like this in my writing or in a student's writing: "Before going on to a discussion of X, it is important to consider Y." The question, of course, is: Why is it important? What is there about Y that makes it a prerequisite to understanding X? Often enough, I find that I do not know (or my student does not know) how X relates to Y. In order to make this connection we have to go back and re-examine the ideas in each passage. Sometimes this examination leads to a clear transitional word; sometimes it leads us to drop an entire passage or move it to some other point in our writing.[4]

Audience and Purpose

Another means by which the process of discovery goes on is through an attempt to define our audience and purpose. Let us assume for example that our purpose in writing is to express our feelings on a controversial topic and that our audience is a close, sympathetic friend. In this case, we may reasonably assume that the audience can provide many details and even understand certain relationships, which we need not specify. Our task is to examine our own attitudes/feelings, identify details which most clearly relate to our perspective, and perhaps associate those details with very personal experiences or feelings. Let us next assume, however, that our task is to persuade, to influence someone else's feelings/attitudes rather than simply to articulate our own point of view. Let us also assume that our audience is skeptical, inclined to play devil's advocate, posing alternative interpretations. Then our problem is to identify that person's values or assumptions and look for facts and arguments that will appear plausible from that perspective. As we consider our audience's values and assumptions,

---

[3]See Richard Beach's study (1976) of the revision strategies of "extensive revisers" and "nonrevisers."

[4]Gabriel Della-Piana (1978) has proposed both a research procedure and a theoretical base for studying the changes writers make in successive drafts of a piece of writing.

we may find ourselves abandoning or at least revising our original point of view.[5]

Cognitive Processes

One more way that the process of discovery goes on is through a deliberate attempt to engage in some of the conscious cognitive processes that constitute "thinking." Two basic assumptions lead me to discuss a few of these processes in some detail. The first assumption is that some of the cognitive activities that enable one to understand a subject are the same activities that enable one to formulate and support the assertions one makes in one's writing. Again, I must stress that we cannot guarantee that the use of these cognitive processes will inevitably lead students to make perceptive, carefully thought-out assertions about the topics on which they write. But if we agree that one feature of good writing is careful consideration of the subject at hand, we can make a second assumption: As we help students engage in basic cognitive activities, we can increase their chances of improving their writing and of understanding the content of our respective disciplines.

For purposes of teaching, I find useful an account of two of these processes in Elbow's (1975) discussion of the "doubting game" and the "believing game" [pp. 147–191].[6] Elbow's basic assumption is that there is *some* perspective from which any assertion (of fact or of value) may seem plausible. One's problem is, first, to play the believing game, to discover the circumstances under which this assertion might seem reasonable or useful. One tries to think of justifications; one empathizes; one tries to find support in one's own experience; one tries to think of comparable assertions or situations which one believes to be true. Even when one disagrees, one looks for possible areas of agreement: common values, experiences, assumptions. Or perhaps one simply listens, paraphrases, summarizes accurately. By contrast, the doubting game entails raising questions, looking for incongruities, thinking of instances in which X is not true, thinking of negative implications, finding counter examples, looking for alternative explanations. In short, *doubting* means doing much of what we call critical thinking. By combining this critical thinking with the believing game, writers can enable themselves to discover what Anatol Rapoport (1960) calls the "region of validity" of an assertion or set of data. By establishing this region of validity, writers may be able to consider novel or confusing or emotionally laden subject matter without

---

[5]Although "audience" has always been important to rhetoricians, we have relatively little research on the way a sense of audience affects either the writing process or product. Charles R. Cooper and I (1976) have suggested procedures that can help researchers determine how a sense of audience may influence a writer's choice of diction, syntax, and content.

[6]These combined activities are comparable to what Anatol Rapoport (1960) refers to as "Rogerian debate."

going to the extremes of uncritical acceptance or mindless rejection of a given viewpoint or body of information.

Under the general rubric of doubting and believing, we can be fairly explicit about the sort of intellectual activity we want students to engage in. The specific terms I propose are scarcely new; my own understanding of them is drawn from tagmemic theory (see Odell, 1977; Young, Becker, & Pike, 1970). I illustrate these terms in order to make sure we do not overlook a powerful set of procedures that, despite their simplicity, can provoke a great variety of questions with which we can examine any subject matter in any discipline.[7]

Contrast:
How is X different from Y (in data at hand; in other data we know about)?
How is X different from what I expected (or hoped or feared or . . . .)?
Is there anything incongruous or self-contradictory about X?
Are there different ways of interpreting X?

Classification:
How can we label X?
What is it similar to
—in our personal experience?
—in fields related to the one we are concerned with?
Is X part of a pattern in the data at hand? Is it an instance of a recurring motif?
If X is part of a pattern, are there subpatterns or subcategories?

Change:
Has X changed? What is it becoming? What could it never become?
If X occurs more than once, does it always occur in the same form or does it vary from instance to instance?

Location in a sequence:
When does X occur? What is the historical setting for X?
What immediately precedes or follows X?
What might cause X? What might X cause?

Location in physical context:
Where does X appear? What is its relation to its surroundings?
How does it affect its surroundings?
How do its surroundings affect it?

We may think of additional questions that engage us and our students in these processes. The point is that as we engage in the basic enterprise of believing and doubting, we need to use contrast, classification, etc.

Although I do not have enough space to consider all the questions I have just

---

[7]We have some evidence (Odell, 1974; Young & Koen, 1973) that tagmemic theory can help students engage in the process of inquiry. However, there are a number of unanswered questions in this area (see Young, 1978; Odell, 1978).

raised, I do briefly illustrate how doubting, believing, and answering some of the questions just raised might help us examine a body of data. In this illustration, my comments may appear more relevant to the process of reading than to the process of writing. This appearance is not coincidental. Most frequently, we ask our students to write about materials they have read. To rephrase my earlier assumption: The act of reading—the act of comprehending, evaluating, analyzing, synthesizing written discourse—requires one to engage in the same cognitive activities that can enable one to formulate the assertions he or she will develop in writing. I would, however, argue that the cognitive processes discussed later are useful in examining many different types of data and are not restricted to the analysis of written discourse. To carry out my illustration, I have chosen passages from John Hersey's *Hiroshima* (1946); the data in this text seem to require little introductory explanation, and the book allows us to raise conceptual problems that appear basic to many different disciplines. To write about this book—i.e., to discover what they wish to say about the book—students must examine a writer's presentation of data; form assertions (of fact, of value) on the basis of that data; and test those assertions.

Here is the passage with which Hersey begins his account of the atomic bombing of Hiroshima:

> At exactly fifteen minutes past eight in the morning, on August 6, 1945, Japanese time, at the moment when the atomic bomb flashed above Hiroshima, Miss Toshiko Sasaki, a clerk in the personnel department of the East Asia Tin Works, had just sat down at her place in the plant office and was turning her head to speak to the girl at the next desk.

Hersey goes on to introduce five other inhabitants of Hiroshima, each engaged in similarly routine activities. After some 15 pages of informatin about these five individuals, Hersey returns to Toshiko Sasaki. He tells us about her day, which began at 3:00 a.m. with Miss Sasaki doing housework and preparing in advance all of the meals her several family members would eat for the rest of the day. Hersey mentions the major events of her morning: her trip to work, her attendance at a meeting to plan a memorial service. After Miss Sasaki leaves the planning meeting, Hersey recounts her actions in some detail.

> Miss Sasaki went back to her office and sat down at her desk. She was quite far from the windows, which were to her left, and behind her were a couple of tall bookcases containing all the books of the factory library, which the personnel department had organized. She settled herself at her desk, put some things in a drawer, and shifted papers. She thought that before she began to make entries in her lists of new employees, discharges, and departures for the Army, she would chat for a moment with the girl at her right. Just as she turned her head away from the windows, the room was filled with a blinding light. She was paralyzed with fear, fixed still in her chair for a long moment (the plant was 1,600 yards from the center).

> Everything fell, and Miss Sasaki lost consciousness. The ceiling dropped suddenly and the wooden floor above collapsed in splinters and the people up there came down and the roof above them gave way; but principally and first of all, the bookcase right behind her swooped forward and the contents threw her down, with her left leg horribly twisted and breaking underneath her. There, in the tin factory, in the first moment of the atomic age, a human being was crushed by books.

Ultimately, I suspect, we will want students to play the doubting game with this book. Powerful and moving as the book is, much of the book's effect depends on Hersey's careful manipulation of data. Without wishing to deny the moral that is implicit in the book, we have to recognize that Hersey presents a very selective picture of the bombing. But to begin, it seems useful to play the believing game, discover what he has done, and identify its region of validity. By this means, we shall see more clearly what he has not done.

To begin examining Hersey's account of the bombing we might focus on Hersey's descriptions of Miss Sasaki, noting the points at which these descriptions recur throughout the book. I have already cited two of these; a third occurs just after she has recovered consciousness, and has recognized that she is buried under a pile of books and debris. One would-be rescuer has tried to rescue her and has given up.

> Much later, several men came and dragged Miss Sasaki out. Her left leg was not severed, but it was badly broken and cut and it hung askew below the knee. They took her out into a courtyard. It was raining. She sat on the ground in the rain. When the downpour increased, someone directed all the wounded people to take cover in the factory's air-raid shelters. "Come along," a torn-up woman said to her. "You can hop." But Miss Sasaki could not move, and she just waited in the rain. Then a man propped up a large sheet of corrugated iron as a kind of lean-to, and took her in his arms and carried her to it. She was grateful until he brought two horribly wounded people—a woman with a whole breast sheared off and a man whose face was all raw from a burn—to share the simple shed with her. No one came back. The rain cleared and the cloudy afternoon was hot; before nightfall the three grotesques under the slanting piece of twisted iron began to smell quite bad.

Hersey's account is so moving that my initial thought is that we must be careful not to murder in order to dissect. But unless we are concerned solely with the aesthetic and affective qualities of an account, the "moving" quality is all the more reason to look closely. One way to begin examining these facts while playing the believing game is to see how the facts relate to each other and to our own understanding of the events Hersey is concerned with. For example, at the very outset of his comments on Miss Sasaki, we are aware of a disparity between the horrible implications of the bomb blast and the innocuous triviality of Miss Sasaki's actions; between Miss Sasaki's limited understanding (Hersey reports that all she was initially aware of was a "blinding light") and our own understanding of what was happening. We might also note contrasts between the treatment any humane reader would want to see her receive and the way she is treated, between what appeared to be true (that the lean-to might give some relief) and what was true (the lean-to ultimately led to her having to endure the sight of two people who were injured even more horribly than was she).

In addition to these contrasts, we might pay particular attention to *change* and *location in sequence*. Early in his narrative, Hersey says that Miss Sasaki was "paralyzed with fear." And that is almost his only reference to changes in feelings. Otherwise, Hersey presents physical, perceptible changes rather than internal, nonperceptible ones. He notes that her leg was broken, that the weather changed. He also comments that the people in her shelter had been horribly wounded, that the "three grotesques... began to smell quite bad." We might especially note the way change and sequence work together here: a change in physical setting occurs at the worst time; it begins to rain hard just at the moment Miss Sasaki is unsheltered; it clears up and becomes warm just at the time when heat will cause her to suffer most. Further, we have to remember that Hersey ends his first chapter with a reference to Miss Sasaki. By doing so, Hersey is able to conclude his chapter with an apparently factual contrast that establishes implicitly his attitude toward the event: "There, in the tin factory, in the first moment of the atomic age, a human being was crushed by books."

In the preceding paragraphs, I have been playing the believing game, describing, appreciatively, the way Hersey has used "facts" to suggest a point of view toward the bombing. I might also have played the believing game by trying to empathize, imagining myself in Miss Sasaki's place or—more realistically— recalling times when I have been at the mercy of events I did not understand and could not control. Further, I could use the events of Hersey's account to support a generalization about the unjustifiability of nuclear war.

This last possibility, however, reminds us of what is at stake in this apparently factual account: issues of morality, of public policy, of the extent and limits of human power. Given these issues, we must play the doubting game. We must consider the limitations of Hersey's account, see if there are reasons we must be cautious of its implications.

It may be hard to find incongruities or paradoxes or self-contradictions within Hersey's text. Also it would be hard to place a different interpretation on the facts presented. Consequently, I want to begin the doubting game by classifying, asking what kinds of data are included and what kinds are excluded.

Put simply, Hersey includes facts that suggest stoicism and in some cases exceptional courage on the part of his six main characters. He does not dwell on any information that might lead us to classify these people as enemies. For example, Hersey tells us that Miss Sasaki works for a tin factory. Presumably, that factory makes some contribution to the war effort, but Hersey gives no information about Miss Sasaki's attitudes toward the war or toward Japan's enemies. I have suggested how skillful Hersey is in his use of sequence. But we must also recognize that Hersey avoids some kinds of questions about sequence: What events preceded the dropping of the bomb? Might any of these events have seemed to justify dropping the bomb? What were the long-range consequences of the bombing? Did the bombing, as was suggested at the time, shorten the war and thereby save lives on both sides?

It is difficult to ask these questions, so moving is Hersey's account, so horrifying are the human implications of the atomic bomb blast. Yet only as we play both the doubting game and the believing game can we form reasonable hypotheses about Hersey's use of data.

As we explore data and form hypotheses, a concern for our ultimate purpose and audience will doubtless have some effect on our process of inquiry. But these latter constraints seem especially important in the process of verifying/testing our hypotheses. Let us assume, for example, that our purpose is to influence our audience's attitude toward Hersey's use of fact and that our audience is not entirely receptive to our point of view. Obviously, we shall have to identify our audience's biases and test our hypotheses by seeing whether they can stand up to and overcome those biases. But let us assume that our purpose is explanatory rather than persuasive and that our audience is not committed to any one view but is inclined to play devil's advocate. In such a case, we test our hypothesis differently. We do not ask: Is my hypothesis adequate to the audience's biases? Rather, we ask: How many other plausible interpretations can I think of? What reasons have I for advancing my hypothesis/interpretation rather than some other? Are there any facts that appear to weaken or discount my hypothesis? How can I modify my hypothesis so as to account for those facts, or what arguments can I find for ignoring these facts? Whether we are trying to explain or to persuade, we test, re-examine, modify our hypotheses. But our sense of audience and purpose leads this process in different directions and implies different criteria for an acceptable hypothesis.

TEACHING THE PROCESS OF DISCOVERY

To summarize my argument thus far: There are several ways in which the process of discovery may take place; among them are the act of writing itself; the attempt to accomplish a given purpose with a particular audience; the conscious attempt to play the believing game and the doubting game and to contrast, classify, etc. In the remainder of this article, I suggest ways we might incorporate the process of discovery into our teaching.

My first suggestion assumes that we need not equate *writing* with long expository essays and research papers. Such writing is important, and I comment on it in a moment. But I want to speak first of short, in-class writing that can serve as an important part of the day-to-day business of understanding the subject matter of a given course. Let us assume, for example, that we want students to think about Hersey's treatment of "factual" material. In a class discussion we might ask students to list 10 or 12 contrasts based on a passage in *Hiroshima*. Assuming that the act of writing can itself be a part of the process of discovery, we might ask students to spend 5 minutes doing what Elbow (1975, pp. 3–11) calls a "free write," in effect an attempt to brainstorm on paper. In these free writes we would ask students to write as rapidly as they could about all the conclusions they might draw from the list of contrasts. We would next ask students to reread their free writes, looking for a center of gravity, a really important assertion that is explicit or implicit in their free writing. Once students have formulated this assertion, they would try to support it on the basis of the list of contrasts on the board or other information in the passage under consideration. After this writing has been completed, we might ask students to read their work aloud and ask other students to play either the doubting game or the believing game. That is, we might ask students to support a classmate's assertions with additional data from the text. Or we might ask students either to think of other, more compelling conclusions about the data at hand, or to look for information in the text that refutes their classmate's assertion.

The activities I have just outlined will take up a good bit of class time. But I suggest that the time will have been well spent, because these activities should have:

—helped students become more comfortable with free writing, a procedure that will, at the very least, enable them to get something down on paper when words do not seem to come readily;

—suggested to students that, by identifying a center of gravity in their free writing, it is possible to learn from one's own writing;

—engaged students in the process of developing a hypothesis on the basis of a set of data, a process that they will go through in many of their college courses;

—introduced students to the doubting game and the believing game, two useful procedures for exploring any topic;

—engaged students in a close examination of some of the subject matter for our course.

The day-to-day in-class activities I have been describing should help students understand what they need to do in writing longer, out-of-class essays. But, because we work with any given group of students for a relatively short time, I am unwilling to leave it to students to make this connection between daily class work and the writing of a longer paper. Thus I think we will need to design classwork specifically to help students understand the intellectual work demanded by a given writing assignment.

Part of this understanding can come from the way we pose the assignment, especially if the assignment helps students identify their audience and purpose. Consider, for example, this assignment from a freshman history course:

Suppose that you had never heard of Edward Bellamy's *Looking Backward*. One day, while killing time in the college library, you came across a dusty, mutilated copy of the book. As you began to read *Looking Backward,* it seemed reasonable for you to guess, although you could find no date of publication, that the book had to be written after a certain date and probably before another date.

What is the narrowest time frame that you would choose? Defend your choice with specific references to customs, institutions, inventions, concepts, or anything else that Bellamy mentions. Document your choice by citing information you found in encyclopedias.

The students' purpose in writing seems clear enough; they are to make an inference about the book and explain their bases for making this inference. They are not simply to express their reactions to the book, nor are they to change the reader's mind about the book; one could disagree with their conclusion about the date of the book and still agree that they had arrived at a well-reasoned hypothesis about when the book was published. There is no explicit statement about the audience, but the term *defend* suggests a healthy skepticism on the part of the reader. The audience here is, of course, the teacher, and the day-to-day work of the course could provide an introduction to that audience—especially if the teacher is likely to conduct class discussions by asking such questions as: What basis do you have for saying that X is true? Why could not Y be equally true? How would you refute the claim of someone who says that Z is true?

As students begin to get a sense of their audience for this essay, they should also begin to get a sense of the sort of thinking they will need to do in order to discover the conclusion they will present in their essays. Certainly a sense of the audience plus the assignment itself suggests that students will need to:

> —cite specific facts from the book;
> —cite more than one kind of fact (not just customs but also, say, inventions);
> —distinguish between anomalous and typical facts;
> —consider alternate conclusions and explain how those conclusions are less satisfactory than one's own conclusion.

From my perspective—unembarrased by any firsthand knowledge of the particular course in which *Looking Backward* was being read—these activities should be part of the day-to-day work of the history class. But at the very least, I would recommend spending one or two class periods in which students examined data (diaries, letters, chronicles) that posed problems comparable to those students would encounter in examining *Looking Backward*. This would let us illustrate the procedures we want students to use in their essays, and it would also let us explain the criteria by which we plan to judge the assertions students make in their essays. Having made these criteria explicit, we should do what we can to insure that students revise their work carefully before turning it in. Specifically, I recommend that, several days before the final draft or the paper is due, we require students to bring to class a complete draft of their paper. During this class session, I think we should do at least two things. First, we should ask the entire class to examine a piece of student writing done in response to the assignment students are working on. (To obtain this writing I usually identify students who I suspect will have fairly strong drafts and ask them to let me ditto passages from their essays.) In examining this writing we would ask students to: (1) form criteria; (2) identify strengths and weaknesses in the passage we are examining; and (3) suggest what the writer needs to do in order to eliminate these weaknesses.

Having gone through this procedure with the class, we might instruct students to revise their own work in the light of work done in class. Or we might have pairs of students exchange papers and use criteria developed in class to make detailed comments on their classmates' papers. Students would consider these comments in preparing a final draft of their papers. If we have little class time to devote to this sort of work, we might ask pairs of students to begin this work in the last few minutes of class time and continue it outside of class.

Once students have turned in their finished drafts, I have only one further recommendation: When we grade students' papers, we must play fair. We must not introduce extraneous criteria. If, for example, we have taught students to base their argument on representative (rather than anomalous) details and to anticipate and refute a reader's objections, we must approach their writing with two questions: How consistently have they chosen representative rather than anomalous details? Have they identified and refuted potential objections? For other assignments, we might ask different questions: Am I moved by this writing? Did I get a good sense of the writer's personality? But for any assignment we should hold students responsible for answering only the questions we have told them we would ask.

CONCLUSION

Although I tried to begin this presentation by establishing some areas of agreement, I must conclude by acknowledging substantial areas of potential disagreement. There is, after all, a student attitude toward writing that can be expressed: "Leave me alone. I'll take my chances." And then, too, all of us have some—a few, one or two—students who write reasonably well, and there are plenty of colleagues who will help us try to find someone to blame for the generally low quality of our other students' writing. Furthermore, an attempt to act upon any of my recommendations may require us to modify our teaching and almost certainly will require us to experience hard work and frustration as we undergo our own process of learning, our own process of identifying the conceptual demands of a given assignment and of devising ways to help students meet those demands. It would, all things considered, be simpler to rail against television or the permissiveness of society or the inadequacy of the education students experienced before they entered our classes.

On the other hand, we are not helpless. If we cannot make immediate changes in our society or our educational system, we have good reason to think that, admittedly with some effort, we can help students gain some control of the processes of discovery in writing and that instruction in those processes can improve the quality of students' writing. And finally, we have some reason to think it may be possible to relate the process of writing to the process of learning a given subject matter. This last possibility alone should make the effort worthwhile—for us and for our students.

REFERENCES

Beach, R. Self-evaluation strategies of extensive revisers and nonrevisers. *College Composition and Communication,* 1976, *27,* 160–164.

Cooper, C. R., & Odell, L. Considerations of sound in the composing process of published writers. *Research in the Teaching of English,* 1976, *10,* 103–115.

Della-Piana, G. Research strategies for the study of revision processes in writing poetry. In C. R. Cooper & L. Odell (Eds.), *Research on composing: Points of departure.* Urbana, Ill.: National Council of Teachers of English, 1978.

Elbow, P. *Writing without teachers.* New York: Oxford University Press, 1975.

Emig, J. Writing as a mode of discovery. *College Composition and Communication,* 1977, *28,* 122–128.

Hersey, J. R. *Hiroshima.* New York: A. A. Knopf, 1946.

Murray, D. Internal revision: A process of discovery. In C. R. Cooper & L. Odell (Eds.), *Research on composing: Points of departure.* Urbana, Ill.: National Council of Teachers of English, 1978. (a)

Murray, D. Teach the motivating force of revision. *English Journal,* 1978, *67*(7), 56–60. (b)

Odell, L. Measuring the effect of instruction in pre-writing. *Research in the Teaching of English,* 1974, *8,* 228–240.

Odell, L. Measuring changes in intellectual processes as one dimension of growth in writing. In C. R. Cooper & L. Odell (Eds.), *Evaluating writing: Describing, measuring, judging.* Urbana, Ill.: National Council of Teachers of English, 1977.

Odell, L. Another look at tagmemic theory. *College Composition and Communication,* 1978, *29,* 146–152.

Rapoport, A. *Fights, games, and debates.* Ann Arbor, Mich.: The University of Michigan Press, 1960.

Young, R. E. Paradigms and problems: Needed research in rhetorical invention. In C. R. Cooper & L. Odell (Eds.), *Research on composing: Points of departure.* Urbana, Ill.: National Council of Teachers of English, 1978.

Young, R. E., Becker, A. L., & Pike, K. L. *Rhetoric: Discovery and change.* New York: Harcourt, Brace & World, 1970.

Young, R. E., & Koen, F. M. *The tagmemic discovery procedure: An evaluation of its uses in teaching rhetoric.* University of Michigan, Grant No. EO5238-71-116, National Endowment for the Humanities, 1973.

8 A Garden of Opportunities and a Thicket of Dangers

Erwin R. Steinberg
Carnegie-Mellon University

At the conclusion of his essay on "Models and Archetypes" in his book *Models and Metaphors,* Max Black (1962) says that if his analysis has been right

> some interesting consequences follow for the relations between the sciences and the humanities. All intellectual pursuits, however different their aims and methods, rely firmly upon . . . exercises of the imagination. . . . Similar archetypes play their parts in different disciplines; a sociologist's pattern of thought may also be the key to understanding a novel. So perhaps those interested in excavating the presuppositions and latent archetypes of scientists may have something to learn from the industry of literary critics [pp. 242–243].

And literary critics and teachers of composition have much to learn from Max Black and from scientists, especially from scientists who propose to test the paradigms by which critics and teachers try to teach others to be literary critics and writers. The relationship can be symbiotic, for, as Black explains, "Perhaps every science must start with metaphor and end with algebra; and perhaps without the metaphor there would never have been any algebra [p. 242]."

Furthermore, I would argue, the practices of the professor of English (a specialist in metaphor) and the professor of psychology (in Black's formula, the algebraist) in fact overlap sufficiently to provide a natural bridge. The English professor is not entirely ignorant of the methodologies and virtues of empirical research; and, as Black (1962) explains, "To speak of 'models' in connection with a scientific theory [as of course, scientists—including psychologists, and especially cognitive psychologists—do] already smacks of the metaphorical [p. 219]."

155

I should like here to take advantage of my position as someone who teaches English (including composition and technical writing) and who dabbles in psychology (sometimes with the approval of the Department of Psychology) to presume to raise with my colleagues in both disciplines a few cautions and a few questions to help us avoid some reinventing of the wheel, defending of turf, exploring of blind alleys, or building of Procrustean beds. What follows, then, is an exploration of some of the ideas raised at the Carnegie-Mellon symposium, the opportunities they offer for further research, and some possible pitfalls in undertaking—or not undertaking—that research.

OUR INHERITANCE

Let me begin by saying that to me probably the most important point made at the symposium was that the teaching of writing focuses too much on product, on the written paper that the student submits, and not enough on process, on how to write. It might be helpful here to examine briefly some of the reasons. In the first place, when a student hands in a paper, there it is and it must be dealt with. And one reacts to it much the way an art critic reacts to a painting or a music critic to a new musical composition: as a work completed, presented. The discussions at the meeting, furthermore, demonstrated that many of us have only been paying lip service to the idea of teaching "composing." Neither the traditional method of outlining, for example, nor what until recently has passed for problem solving serves the writer adequately in what we are now calling the pre-writing stage (the stage rhetoricians call "invention"). Neither is an adequate model of the processes most writers employ.

We are also, as Richard Young pointed out in our discussions at this symposium, the inheritors of a romantic model that urges that truly creative writing is mysterious and nonrational, the result, ultimately, of inviting the muse rather than of employing consciously an ordered, rational process. Unfortunately, that tradition is still strong, and we have to make clear that we don't desert or besmirch the muse when we teach some kind of logical approach to planning or pre-writing.

Ultimately, however, the problem has been that teachers of writing have not had a useful alternative to the romantic model to propose to their students nor the tools to develop one. The psychologists were no help, because by the time the problem of teaching writing had become widespread enough to merit serious attention, psychology, in an attempt to become scientific, had become behavioristic. Concepts like "mind," "consciousness," and even "image," and the techniques of the Würzburg school developed to examine "mental processes" were not only shunned by psychologists, but denounced. Fortunately, the cognitive psychologists, with their use of protocols and their more rigorous terminology, have begun to provide new methodologies and are now proposing new models that invite serious attention. After listening to these papers and then reading them, I understand that the proposed models are still tentative and the proposers themselves open to suggestions and advice of all kinds. If professors of English refuse to involve themselves with their development, they will be taking the same sort of stance that resulted in the delivery of rhetoric to departments of speech some generations back—a rejection that the discipline of English has only recently begun to recognize as a serious error.

THE CURRENT MODELS AS A BEGINNING

As teachers of writing listened to the models proposed at the symposium, some of them raised a variety of objections—that, for example, the teaching of writing should take into consideration not only the need for rigor, but also sensitivity to historical precedent, allusiveness, subtlety, and eloquence; that the study of writing is a liberal study that should go beyond the teaching of what might seem to be an unimaginative series of orderly steps; that one must not neglect the ethics of what is written in the teaching of writing.

All these things may be true, but they are not really relevant to the models proposed. First, the use of any model need not preclude consideration of allusiveness, subtlety, eloquence, or any other matters that the teacher normally raises with students. Use of a model does not rule out everything—or anything— that the teacher now does. Second, the models that we have seen have focused so far largely on pre-writing, with the writing and editing stages only broadly sketched in. And pre-writing is what teachers of composition know least about. Furthermore, as I understand the "search procedures" proposed in these models as heuristics, they will promote subtlety by providing the writer with a wider understanding of his or her problem and a wider range of specific detail to use in his or her writing. And as for eloquence, that will come in a later stage—most likely if professors of English remain involved in what is now a common enterprise, perhaps less likely if they withdraw. As J. R. Hayes said during the discussion, we are dealing with an "ill-defined problem." Such problems must first be parsed to determine interacting subsets, the subsets must then be dealt with individually, and then the interactions must be studied. As I understand it, we are still parsing and dealing with some of the early subsets in the process. Third, because research in this area is just beginning, the models that we have seen may be somewhat naive, especially to English teachers who daily are faced with the full complexity of teaching seventeen- and eighteen-year-olds how to write. But people doing research in cognitive processes have to reduce the operations they are studying to their simplest possible terms in order to begin to understand them. After they map out the basic design of a process, they can add and map increasing orders of complexity. That was the way, for example, cognitive psychologists undertook the study of playing chess. The fact that on the one hand we have developed at Carnegie-Mellon University a good computer program for playing chess against competent human chess players, and that on the other our psychologists and computer people know that it is not good enough and continue to improve it, is evidence that they understand the danger of reductionism.

Furthermore, if anyone is disturbed by the naiveté or seeming poverty of the models we have seen so far, he or she can improve them by adding heuristics that will enable or even require the writer to consider early such matters as historical precedent or ethics. As I understand it, no one has yet offered us anything that comes close to being a definitive model. Although the pre-writing models that we have seen have gone through several stages of increasing complexity, I have heard no one suggest that even the pre-planning stage has been adequately mapped.

DANGERS OF UNCRITICAL ACCEPTANCE

Having mentioned the apparent naiveté of the models of writing that are currently available, I should also say a word about the naiveté of what we think we know. Each of us "knows" a good bit about how to write and about how to teach writing. But it does not take much reading in the literature to demonstrate that many of our peers "know" not only a variety of other similar truths, but even a variety of truths that flatly contradict ours. Furthermore, many of us are old enough to remember when most teachers "knew" that not only the best way at the time but the best conceivable way to describe how the English language functions was to use traditional grammar. More of us remember when the best conceivable and in fact the definitive description was thought to be structural linguistics. I haven't heard similar claims about transformational-generative grammar, but I would assume that some people at least are making them.

It behooves us to be modest about what we "know" and not to object when someone puts that knowledge to a rigorous test, a test more rigorous than one can apply in a regular classroom.

Similarly, it behooves those doing the needed research to consider what the experienced teachers of composition have to suggest. That is the best place for them to find metaphors useful to be turned into the needed algebra. They will want, of course, to begin with some of the simpler metaphors; but I can promise them that many of the more exotic ones will also suggest useful directions.

I would not, however, suggest that either teachers or researchers adopt proposed models uncritically; and I am particularly concerned about the uncritical acceptance of ideas that seem already to have been adopted with less than rigorous scrutiny.

Is Writing Always a Process of Discovery?

For example, one widely accepted bit of knowledge that I'd like to see tested is the idea—now become a cliché—that one doesn't really know what one means until one has said or written it. Lee Odell has told us in his chapter that for him writing is a process of discovery. I believe him. But John Gould, in his chapter, questions the validity of the idea that one doesn't really know what one means until he or she has written it. Because this is a very important matter for teachers of writing, I'd like to explore it here.

I discover what I mean as I write only in situations where I am suddenly forced to write immediately. In situations where I have time to think about the writing problem, which is most of the time, I generally do not sit down to write until I have thought through reasonably well pretty much what I want to say, roughly the order in which I want to say it, and certainly the conclusions I wish to draw. There are, of course, sometimes surprises along the way, but not as a general rule. I find, furthermore, that when I try to force myself to write before I have thought through what I want to say, when I try to write before I am "ready," it is very difficult and I usually give up. When I am "ready," however, the words and sentences pour out.

Frequently my thinking during pre-writing will include making notes. If I am planning to answer a letter, for example, I will make quick notes in the margins of that letter and, if my reply is to be a long one, will number items so that when I write or dictate I will have a guide to the order that I want to use. When I write a paper, I usually have one or more sheets on which I write short notes, generally less than sentence length, so that I won't forget various aspects of the paper that I've thought about or thought through.

I work with those notes before writing, scratching out some, combining others, changing still others; but I do it all on the original page or pages and move directly from that stage to writing without an intermediate stage of writing an outline. My first drafts, of course, have to be augmented and edited, but when I am through polishing, I seldom have a piece of writing that is significantly different from what I had in mind before I started to write it.

Sometimes one can think through a writing problem without making any notes and, indeed, without using much language in the "thinking." Imagine the following situation. You have been assigned to write for the occupants of a particular floor of a particular building instructions on how to use a newly installed fire escape. Standing across the street, you watch as one of the installers demonstrates how it works. He opens the lone window on the north wall of the building, steps out on the metal platform, moves diagonally right to a large crank, lifts and swings left and down a locking bar, and turns the crank clockwise, lowering a stairlike section of the fire escape. When the bottom of the stairs touches the ground, he pulls a red handle to the right of the crank, dropping a locking pin in place, and descends to the street. He says nothing to you during the procedure. To review the procedure in your mind preparatory to writing it, you imagine yourself going through it. You picture yourself reaching out to raise the window, raising the window, and then stepping out onto the fire escape—and you not only "see" these actions in your mind but "feel" them as well. You then "see" and "feel" yourself moving diagonally to the right to the crank, reaching out with your left hand to raise and swing left and down the locking bar, and then turning the crank clockwise as you watch and listen for the ladder to reach the ground. Finally, you "see" and "feel" yourself reaching out with your right hand to drop the locking pin.

As I went through that imaginary episode in my own mind, preparatory to writing the two—duplicating—preceding scenes, very few words were involved: faintly "window," "crank," and "ladder." I was much more aware of the tension in my muscles as I imagined myself raising the window and the "feeling" of the shifting of weight from the ball of my left foot to the ball of my right as I stepped over the window sill onto the fire escape. I thus stored the entire procedure in my mind largely as a series of visual and kinesthetic images.

I think that in every sense of the meaning of the phrase, I "knew what I meant" to say about the procedure before I translated it into the language I used earlier. Similarly, there are many times in writing when I reject a particular sentence, phrase, or word not because I am feeling for exactly what I mean but because I know what I mean and have not yet found the appropriate language to express it. It is as though I have a template in my mind for which I must find the matching language.

Finally, examine this paragraph from a business memo that was submitted to me recently:

> Peoria informed the Tele-Computer Center that regular customers have been merged. Mr. Wright provided Mr. Young with a list of the accounts which have been merged. Mr. Young is in the process of reviewing this list. It appears that some merging has been accomplished but accounts remain that need to be merged. Mr. Young will work with Peoria to identify and merge the remaining accounts.

It is clear that what the writer of that statement "meant" is:

> After someone in the Peoria office informed the Tele-Computer Center that accounts of regular customers had been merged, Mr. Wright provided Mr. Young with a list of merged accounts which Mr. Young is reviewing. Because a sample checking of that list against the master file proved that some of the merging has in fact not yet been completed, Mr. Young will work with the Peoria office to identify and merge the remaining accounts.

The order and juxtaposition of ideas in the original paragraph make clear that what was intended was what I provided in the revision. Thus in some real sense, the writer of the original "knew" what he meant without ever having adequately translated that meaning into language.

Note that I am not saying that muddled writing is not frequently the result of muddled thinking, of the writer's not being clear about what is meant or even not understanding the subject. That frequently is true. And, indeed, giving students a writing assignment is a useful device to help them think through what they "mean"—or should "mean"—about the concept of "work" in physics or the concept of "revolution" in history or the concept of "archetype" in literary criticism. But extrapolating such occurrences into the dictum that one never really knows what one means until one has said or written it is, I firmly believe, carrying an idea to its illogical conclusion. I would like to see someone set up an experiment to test my contention.

I should also point out here that much of the evidence given in support of the "writing as discovery" thesis frequently comes from poets, dramatists, and novelists. Thus, for example, in a paper on "Internal Revision: A Process of Discovery," Donald M. Murray describes how, listening to a lecture one day, he found himself "doodling with language"; and, he continues (Cooper & Odell, 1978):

> I have followed this short story for only a couple of pages in the past few days. I am ashamed to reveal the lines above [i.e., his "doodling," which he quotes]—I don't know if they will lead me to a story—but I'm having fun and think I should share this experience, for it is revealing of the writing process [p. 89].

Elsewhere in his paper, Murray offers supporting evidence for his views from writers like Neil Simon, Dylan Thomas, and Archibald MacLeish, and he appends to the end of his article claims from writers that, as Edward Albee, the first writer on the list, puts it (Cooper & Odell, 1978): "Writing has got to be an act of discovery. . . . I write to find out what I'm thinking about [pp. 101–103]." Again, however, the evidence is from "creative" rather than expository writers: Of the 47 writers in the appended list, I have been able to identify 40—and all are dramatists, novelists, or poets.

In the first place, however, even with all the evidence that Murray provides, I would question whether the process he is recommending is universally true for, let us say, good novelists. Joseph Heller, for example, used a very elaborate chart in writing *Catch-22* on which he plotted the various episodes in the novel (Kiley & McDonald, 1973, cover and pp. 1, 41, 271, 307, and 333). He recently reported (Gelb, 1979), "I get an opening line, and a concept of the book as a full, literary entity. It's all in my head before I even begin to write [p. 55]." Like Heller, Emil Zola made extensive plans for *Germinal,* which he followed carefully in the writing of that novel (Grant, 1970). And we have the following testimony from Virginia Woolf (1954):

> Meanwhile, before I can touch the *Jessamy Brides,* I will have to write my book on fiction and that won't be done till January, I suppose. And it is possible that the idea will evaporate. Anyhow this records the odd horrid unexpected way in which these things suddenly create themselves—one thing on top of another in about an hour. So I made up *Jacob's Room* looking at the fire at Hogarth House; so I made up the *Lighthouse* one afternoon in the Square here [pp. 104–105].

Clearly, then, unlike Edward Albee, many writers know "what they are thinking about" before they get to the actual writing of a piece of fiction.

But more important, what may be true for many writers of poems, plays, and novels is not necessarily true for writers of exposition intended to communicate. I can best proceed with my analysis here by analogy. I have seen an artist rub a length of charcoal across a piece of paper and go on to develop a very interesting drawing from the suggestions in the accidental qualities of that original smudge. I have also seen an artist paint the left-hand side of a canvas, move on to the right-hand side of that canvas, and then return to redo completely the left-hand side of the canvas as a result of what he had done on the right-hand side. I have been told—and can understand—that a piece of sculpture can be as much or more the result of the grain or shape of the piece of wood or stone that the sculptor chooses to work on as of any original conception that the sculptor may have. I know that, similarly, a poet can begin a poem with a single image that has some-how popped into his or her mind and that he or she has read somewhere, a drama-tist or novelist can begin a play or novel with a particular character or set of characters or with a particular scene in mind—and from such beginnings move on to "discover" as he or she writes what becomes the final poem, play, or novel.

Furthermore, it has long been accepted that poets use language in a way that calls attention to the language itself, rather than only to what the language signifies; and in our century novelists have adopted the same aesthetic stance. Thus, although as a young man James Joyce (1968) announced that "The artist, like the God of the creation, remains within or beyond or above his handiwork, invisible, refined out of existence, indifferent, paring his fingernails [p. 215]," by the time he got to the writing of the middle of *Ulysses* he had clearly rejected that proposition and was writing in a way that called attention more and more to his virtuosity in the use of language, and thus to himself as the writer (Steinberg, 1973). Any page of *Finnegans Wake* will demonstrate how the modern novelist can "play" with language in very much the same way that a composer plays with a set of notes or the poet a set of images.

For the writer of a proposal for a grant or a report on research, however, such virtuosity is counterproductive. Language is used to communicate—to explain, inform, persuade. In such instances, language that calls attention to itself im-pedes communication. The writing process of the proposal or report writer is also different from that of the poet or novelist. The central idea for the annual report from a department chairman, for example, seldom begins with an image, which then exfoliates as the muse allows. Procedures for expository writing are typi-cally much more orderly.

In the process of writing, report writers do sometimes "discover" a new way to say something, a useful analogy, a felicitous phrase, or even a better way to organize a particular section than they had originally planned, but I wouldn't have much faith in a report writer who sat down to write a report with only the equivalent of a poetic image or a character or a scene in mind. Having done the research, he or she will thus have done much—although of course not all—of the pre-writing.

I tell you all this not because I want to persuade you that writing cannot be a process of discovery. Clearly for some people it is. We know that it is for Lee Odell and for others at the symposium and elsewhere. Indeed, as I have said, it has become a cliché—for people at this symposium and writers of papers about teaching composition. I see it, however, as a serious overgeneralization and as an example of how important it is that we test our intuitively derived models.

How Many Models?

We must always be careful not to think in terms of a single model, because if we do we'll find one and force everyone to use it—the way English teachers used to require students to make formal outlines before they wrote. For some people, a particular method may work, even work well, but perhaps not for all people. Furthermore, in insisting that all students use a particular method, English teachers frequently teach those students to cheat: Many students who are required to submit outlines with their themes write the paper first and then develop the outline from it; they imply, however, or even say, when they hand the outline and paper in together, that they wrote the outline first.

Another matter that must be looked into is the place of revision in expository writing. Many teachers of writing see it as the most important step in the writing process. Donald Murray, for example, begins the paper I have already referred to with the statement (Cooper & Odell, 1978), "Writing is rewriting [p. 85]." But the evidence offered by John Gould in Chapter 5 of this volume leads him to conclude that "Heavy revision may be limited to 'professional' writing—as done by professional authors . . . or people . . . whose careers are directly affected by how they formulate and communicate their thoughts in writing, oftentimes to large, diverse, and relatively unknown audiences." Once again, different kinds of writing may require different models.

So may different kinds of writers. After more than 30 years of teaching writing both to college freshmen, including engineering freshmen, and to engineers and managers in industry, I continue to be impressed with how different the concerns and needs of the two groups are. Thus even when basic models of cognitive processes in writing have been developed to the point that high school and college teachers of writing will feel that it will be profitable to take them into the classroom, there will still be problems of teaching writing to other groups.

Take, for example, a report I have just finished reading: an electrical engineer explaining an electrical failure in a mine, which resulted in the loss of a complete shift. Before he ever looked into the problem, he knew about generators, trans-formers, circuits, bus bars, switchgear, and circuit breakers. Drawings of the electrical system at the mine gave him the necessary specific details to under the investigation, as a result of which he isolated three possible causes: moisture and atmospheric conditions, a loose bolt at the connection on a bus bar, or an improper cable termination. Even if one argues that his investigation was part of the pre-writing stage of his report, it is clear that that investigation was guided—even directed—by his earlier training and experience. Furthermore, the problem he was examining was carefully circumscribed: a particular electrical failure in a particular mine.

Now take most college freshmen in a composition class. Few of them have studied or experienced deeply enough in any area to be able to analyze a problem of the kind I have just described.

It is frequently argued that we can provide topics about which freshmen do in fact have considerable experience: the relationship of parents and children, for example, or what the students expect in their relationship with the opposite sex. It is true that most students are thoroughly experienced in such relationships. But it is also true that such matters are as open-ended as the electrical engineer's problem was neatly circumscribed. Furthermore, although most students have experienced such relationships, many of them deeply, or even traumatically, it is also true that such relationships are difficult for most people to deal with at any age and that college freshmen are at an age when such relationships are most confusing.

Even asking freshmen to write about problems stemming from a particular novel or piece of nonfiction raises similar difficulties. First, most of them are not skillful enough readers to be able to glean from their reading the necessary details to solve the problem posed; and second, the problem posed is likely to be as open-ended and as fraught with psychological and philosophic difficulties as problems stemming from their own lives.

Motivation is another aspect of the writing process that assumes varying degrees of importance at different times in a person's life. Professionals in industry, for example, understand the importance of writing, and I have to expend relatively little effort to motivate them. With college freshmen, however, motivation is a continual problem. Presenting college students with a model that will make writing easier and more successful will ameliorate that problem, but it will never solve it completely.

I have gone into this difference between "real-world" writing and freshmen writing in such detail to argue that we should be careful not to assume that cognitive models of "real-world" writers will necessarily be useful to freshmen—or vice versa. If the analysis I have just gone through is correct, models for freshmen, to be useful, will have to pay much more attention to heuristics for developing both specific details and the generalizations to be derived from them than will models for "real-world" writers.

Another problem that was raised at the symposium and should be examined is whether, as people grow older, their ability to write develops in clear, perhaps even Piagetian, stages. Carl Bereiter's Chapter 4 in this volume indicates that an important step in this direction has already been taken. We need to know, for example, whether the models being developed or the models that will be developed will be appropriate not only in college but also in high school, junior high school, and elementary school; or whether several sets of models will have to be developed to accommodate the needs, competencies, and levels of understanding of students at two, three, or even four or more stages of the educational ladder. Bereiter's chapter suggests the latter.

We must also examine the differences between good and bad models, the varieties of each, and how and when to use each. We certainly ought to ascertain models used by good writers; but when we do, will we find one, or three, or thirty-three? And if we find more than four or five, how many do we teach? And if we teach one or more, how do we avoid turning them into meaningless formulas or Procrustean beds—two teaching problems that are always with us? Will we find clearly different types of models of bad writing, and if so, how many? And will it be profitable to discuss certain of such models in the classroom because they are typical of what many students do?

NEEDED RESEARCH BEYOND
THE BASIC MODELS

Once the basic cognitive models of writing are available, other kinds of cognitive and curriculum research will become necessary. For example, it would be very useful to know whether it would be more helpful to assign first writing problems that require the students simply to summarize what they know or have learned (what Linda Flower calls writer-based prose) or to assign writing problems that require them to inform or instruct a specific audience (what Flower calls reader-based prose).

In various discussions of writing models that I have read or in which I have been involved, there have been suggestions that a good way to teach students to write is to assign a problem first in a way that requires them simply to summarize what they know and then, as a second step, to assign a revision of the piece of writing for a particular audience, that is, to require first a piece of writer-based prose and then ask that it be rewritten into reader-based prose. Research may prove me wrong, but at the moment I would argue against such a practice. Students will resent having to write what they feel is the same paper twice, and they will find it difficult. Once one has woven a set of ideas into a particular design, it is not easy to unweave and reweave into a new design. Furthermore, I don't think that's the way people really write. In my experience, people who write well use their audience as a generator of ideas, as a constraint (i.e., a filter), and as a means of organizing; and I think that we ought to teach writing that way from the beginning.

Posing reasonable audiences is not as simple as it sounds. On the one hand, the audience should be specific enough to govern what facts the writer uses and what the tone and thrust of the written statement should be. On the other, the audience should not be so exotic as to invite laughter or irritation. I can remember a period here at Carnegie-Mellon University when, in our zeal for teaching problem solving in writing courses, we posited such bizarre audiences that we annoyed our students instead of motivating them. In one assignment, for example, we asked students to write an explanation of the use of the toothbrush for a native of the Canadian Arctic region who had never seen one. As an exercise, it has interesting possibilities; and with students of some maturity it might be recognized as a game from which one might learn. But college freshmen are not notably mature. In one class, for example, it was clear that the students were moving from amusement to annoyance when one day about midsemester I came into the room at the beginning of the hour and saw on the board something like the following: "Write an explanation for a one-armed paper hanger who is allergic to paste about how he can paper this room while standing on one foot without harming the newly shellacked floor."

Similarly, we need to know more about other aspects of teaching writing and of making writing assignments: how best and how often to involve the entire class in the group employment of the various heuristics of preplanning for demonstration in class, with the use of the blackboard, of how they work; when to assign writing problems in stages and when to assign them whole; how to involve teachers in various subject matters to concern themselves with the writing of their students.

There were various points made in papers and in the various discussions at the symposium that should also be tested. There was, for example, the suggestion of using writing as an instrument of learning by periodically assigning short papers to require students to crystalize their ideas about a particular set of lessons or a particular unit before moving on. Perhaps one could employ here the distinction that testing specialists make between formative and summative evaluation and resist grading such papers, considering them not tests but useful way stations for the students at which they look back over where they have come and make sure they understand the map that they have been using. For the teacher these papers could serve as a method of discovering whether in fact all the students have made it to the way station and whether some of them need further training in dealing with certain kinds of terrain or with certain aspects of map reading. Such papers could be considered opening statements in a dialogue between individual students and the teacher, a dialogue continued by written responses by the teacher on the student's paper or in a conference, or both—but a dialogue in which the teacher does not formally evaluate.

At the symposium, Marlene Scardamalia talked about using groups of peer readers, students reading each other's papers, so that the teacher is not overwhelmed by having to read and comment on everything that each student writes.

I have frequently been tempted to try such a procedure but have never been able to overcome the guilt feelings involved. The result is that when I have tried it, I have wound up reading and commenting not only on the original papers but on the peer-group comments as well. If research will show that periodic peer-group readings and comments are adequate and that students learn from them, I'd be happy to relax somewhat my painful Puritanism.

Several people at the symposium also raised the matter of the relation of reading and writing. Are "good" writers "better" readers than "poor" writers? If so, in what sense? If we improve a student's ability to read, will it then be easier to teach him or her to write? Might that, in fact, be a preferred path?

What is the relationship between design in writing and design in the various engineering disciplines or in industrial design or architecture or poetry? Is there available a general concept of design that could be used in the teaching of writing in such a way that the student will understand that the principles of design used in putting together a good letter, essay, or report are similar to the principles of design employed in the student's own discipline? Or does attempting to answer such questions force us to such levels of abstraction that we find ourselves dealing with models of problem solving and not with principles of design at all?

Clearly the research reported on at the Carnegie-Mellon symposium has indicated that much useful work has already been done, but just as clearly there are several generations of profitable research ahead. Both facts should bring satisfaction. I would hope that, as we move over and over from metaphor to algebra in mapping the cognitive processes in writing, we will do so in interdisciplinary cooperation and thus experience some of the "interesting consequences" that Max Black promises will "follow for the relations between the sciences and the humanities."

REFERENCES

Black, M. *Models and metaphors*. Ithaca, N.Y.: Cornell University Press, 1962.

Cooper, C. R., & Odell, L. (Eds.) *Research on composing*. Urbana, Ill.: National Council of Teachers of English, 1978.

Gelb, B. Catching Joseph Heller. *The New York Times Magazine,* March 1979, p. 55.

Grant, E. M. *Zola's "Germinal."* Leicester: Leicester University Press, 1970.

Joyce, J. [A portrait of the artist as a young man] (C. G. Anderson, Ed.). New York: Viking, 1968. (Originally published in 1912.)

Kiley, F., & McDonald, W. (Eds.) *A "Catch-22" casebook*. New York: Thomas Y. Crowell, 1973.

Steinberg, E. R. *The stream of consciousness and beyond in ULYSSES*. Pittsburgh, Pa.: University of Pittsburgh Press, 1973.

Woolf, V. [A writer's diary] (L. Woolf, Ed.). New York: Harcourt, Brace & World Company, 1954.

Author Index

Italics denote pages with bibliographic information.

Subject Index